I went from laughing to being encouraged by one of the finest pastors in The Wesleyan Church. When I read Mark O. Wilson's writings, I enjoy the spiritual insights of an A. W. Tozer sprinkled with just enough of Garrison Keillor's humor. Enjoy these Spirit-filled insights from the Northwoods.

—Dr. Mark Gorveatte, president, Kingswood University

Mark O. Wilson is a real pastor telling real stories from a real church. Every veteran minister has run on empty or faced seasons of spiritual dryness. This book does not gloss over the causes and the difficulty of ministry today. Mark is a great storyteller, and part way through the book I felt like I had actually accompanied him on house calls and into difficult board meetings. But Mark does not leave us lamenting our dryness, or feeling guilty for feeling guilty. He tosses hope to exhausted ministers and gives fresh ideas to replenish the soul. This is not a how-to book, but a very *spiritual* book at its heart.

—Keith Drury, professor of religion and philosophy, Indiana Wesleyan University

Spoiler Alert! Readers of this new book, *Filled Up, Poured Out* are likely to have their spirits revived and hearts refreshed. Rarely have I found a book where the title *and* subtitle so accurately described my experience as a reader. Mark is personal, vulnerable, refreshing, and timely in his passion for those who serve in ministry leadership to be encouraged of heart, passion, and purpose. Instead of depending on yesterday's grace, Mark urges us to preach, pray, lead, and love through the fullness of Christ's Spirit. This book is not only well written; it is well filled up and poured out. I strongly recommend it.

—Dr. John Jackson, president, William Jessup University

*Filled Up, Poured Out* confronts blockages to the free flow of God's grace and power in our lives and ministries. Even better, it coaches us on how to replenish and release the fullness of the indwelling Spirit of Christ. This is the most uplifting guide for personal renewal and practical holiness that I've come across recently.

—Jerry Pence, General Superintendent, The Wesleyan Church; president, Global Holiness Alliance

The greatest problem we face is leading without spiritual power. Mark has addressed this problem head-on and shares a solid, practical, theological means of defeating this enemy. Readers will truly discover how to revive their passion and fulfill their God-given purposes.

—Nolen Rollins, lead pastor and coach, Legacy Church, Estero, Florida

This is a wonderfully engaging text that grabs the reader's attention with the first paragraph. And it is much more than another volume in the genre of devotional literature. Wilson writes in the grand tradition of Wesleyan spirituality that begins with John Wesley himself.

—Ruth Tucker, teacher, author, conference speaker

Refreshing and inspiring, *Filled Up, Poured Out* will revive the spirits of pastors and church leaders and help them minister from the overflow of God's presence.

—Mark Batterson, lead pastor, National Community Church

*Filled Up, Poured Out* is a wonderful source for spiritual refreshment and renewal. You will be blessed and strengthened as you read and apply the helpful common sense steps to a more satisfying and effective ministry.

—H. B. London, Pastor to Pastors Emeritus, Focus on the Family

This is what the church of Jesus Christ has been waiting for—a call, challenge, and model of Holy-Spirit empowered living that transforms people and communities. This book is a change agent for the church of the second decade of the twenty-first century.

—Dr. Jo Anne Lyon, General Superintendent, The Wesleyan Church

Mark O. Wilson has distilled years of pastoral wisdom, insight, and humor into these pages. His understanding of the history of revivals and love for the Wesleyan tradition gives this book a rare combination of spiritual and theological insight—packaged in words and stories accessible to everyone. This is the right book at the right time; pastors, youth, and adults will all benefit from learning how to revive their passion and purpose.

—Rev. Tom Albin, dean of Upper Room Ministries and
director of Ecumenical Relations

*Filled up, Poured Out* is a resignation prevention kit for church leaders. Read its pages and discover insights, challenges, and most of all encouragement from a writer who serves in the ministry trenches. Reading the book was an oasis for my soul.

—Stan Toler, best-selling author; General Superintendent,
Church of the Nazarene

God has used Mark O. Wilson to grow thriving congregations around him and to encourage hundreds of pastors who work in the trenches every day. With his typical humor, hope, and simplicity, Mark gives us the rare insight and illustrations into leadership that can only come from a pastor's heart. May God use this book to encourage thousands more in their personal walk.

—Steve DeNeff, senior pastor, College Wesleyan Church

Mark O. Wilson's *Filled Up, Poured Out* is an easy-to-read, engaging treatise that encourages and challenges Christian leaders to take their faith more seriously in a day when playing church and experiencing ministry burn-out are epidemic. Wilson's uncommon love for Jesus shines brightly through every chapter.

—Frank Viola, author of *Epic Jesus, From Eternity to Here, Revise Us Again,* and *Jesus Manifesto* (with Leonard Sweet)

Pastor Mark is one of those special preachers filled with a humble overflowing of God's love. *Filled Up, Poured Out* is a book you'll want to devour.

—Famous Dave Anderson, restaurateur and keynote speaker

I heartily endorse this book, *Filled Up, Poured Out*. The book has warmed my heart. It has stirred my soul. It will bless and encourage readers everywhere.

—Lareau Lindquist, cofounder, Barnabas International

Mark Wilson's heart for God is contagious. And from engaging stories to practical teaching, *Filled Up, Poured Out* is an invitation for pastors and ministry leaders to be refreshed in the Holy Spirit. Dive in.

—Kevin Myers, senior pastor, 12Stone Church

A great and inspiring book. A must-read for every Christian leader.

—Dr. Philip Griffin, Senior Pastor, Elmbrook Church

# Filled Up, Poured Out

How God's Spirit Can Revive Your
Passion and Purpose

Mark O. Wilson

wesleyan
publishing
house

Indianapolis, Indiana

Copyright © 2012 by Mark O. Wilson
Published by Wesleyan Publishing House
Indianapolis, Indiana 46250
Printed in the United States of America
ISBN: 978-0-89827-527-8

Library of Congress Cataloging-in-Publication Data

Wilson, Mark O.
Filled up, poured out : how God's spirit can revive your passion and purpose /
Mark O. Wilson.
   p. cm.
Includes bibliographical references (p.  ).
ISBN 978-0-89827-527-8
1. Church renewal. 2. Church growth. 3. Church. 4. Holy Spirit. I. Title.
BV600.3.W573 2012
253--dc23
                                    2011041444

In memory of my father, Rev. Andrew Wilson,
who modeled what it means to live in the overflow.

# Contents

# Acknowledgements

Thanks to . . .

- My Savior, Jesus Christ, for being the source and sustainer of holy love.
- Cathy, my lovely bride, for demonstrating the purple grace-truth blend so beautifully. I love you with all my heart.
- Wes, Luke, Ryan, Hannah, and Adam for the fun family experiences and great sermon illustrations. You make me a happy pappy.
- My mother, Elsie Wilson, who embodies missional holiness.
- My big brothers, Wayne, Sam, Steve, and Tim for not selling me to the zoo.
- Phil and Madelyn Crail, the best in-laws ever, and to Gary, Nancy, and Neal for including me.
- Loretta, Ben, Heath, Jeremy, Tim, Linda, Lori, and Donna for faithfully serving together with me in ministry and your patient endurance while I was writing this book. You're the best!
- The Hayward Wesleyan Church family for your loving support and willingness to touch the world from the end of it.

- Steve Gerich, Wayne Richards, Dan Bickel, Ron Gormong, Russell Buck, my small group, and GHAMA and LDJ groups for being dear friends who shepherd my heart and speak wisdom into my life.
- My friend, Charlie, who blesses everybody.
- Keith Drury for writing the book on how to write a book that inspired this book.
- Jerry Pence, Ruth Tucker, Mark Batterson, Larry Ramsell, and Jerry Brecheisen for encouraging my writing.
- Chad, my Nazarene nephew beta-tester. Your grandpa would be proud.
- Orval Butcher, who taught me how to serve the Lord with gladness.
- Ron Carlson, who graciously agreed to review this book for endorsement, but went home to be with Jesus before the final edit.
- General Publisher, Don Cady, for following the inner nudge and initiating this publication.
- Kevin Scott, Rachael Stevenson, Lyn Rayn, Joe Jackson, Nathan Freemyer, and the whole gang at Wesleyan Publishing House. It has been a pleasure partnering with you.

PART 1

# Vacuus

empty, devoid of, free from

O God, you are my God, earnestly I seek you;
my soul thirsts for you, my body longs for you,
in a dry and weary land where there is no water.

—Psalm 63:1

# 1

# Clouds without Rain

## Empty Pastors

## Hitting the Wall

I felt numb. Normally, a long October drive through the scenic
Wisconsin Northwoods refreshed my spirit, but not this day. My
heart was too heavy to notice.

Two weeks earlier, flying home from a speaking engagement
in New Brunswick, I had been weary from a long stretch of fast-
paced and demanding ministry. I looked forward to recharging. My
busy schedule had left my soul running on about an eighth of a
tank, and I knew I needed to fill up again soon.

Then I received a shocking revelation that changed everything.
It was one of those bad-news moments forever frozen in memory.
Melvin and Delores Sipe, the oldest members of my congregation,
had been brutally murdered in their home.

A drug-crazed teenager with ambitions of gang membership forced his way into this elderly couple's house and killed them. The whole community reeled with horror and disbelief. These things occur in big cities. They're not supposed to happen in Norman Rockwell villages like Hayward, Wisconsin.

The Sipes were pillars of our congregation. Hayward Wesleyan Church had been their home ever since Mel's parents joined as charter members in 1925. Our church was the hub of life for Mel and Delores. We were like family and included in their closest circle of friends. Mel, a kindhearted carpenter, crafted our Communion table and the kitchen cabinets. Delores was known to our vacation Bible school children as the cookie lady. Their deaths were a tragedy beyond imagination.

The Sunday following the murders, we cried together and sang old hymns to strengthen each other. Amazingly, a bald eagle came to church that Sunday and perched at the highest point on the sanctuary roof. She stayed there the entire morning. I considered it a postcard from heaven, reminding us of Isaiah 40:31, "They that wait upon the LORD shall renew their strength; they shall mount up with wings as eagles" (KJV).

But, I didn't find an eagle's strength in the days that followed. In fact, I felt weaker as events passed in a blur. My entire schedule was consumed with the funeral, phone calls, dealing with reporters, comforting grieving family members and friends, and trying to make sense of the tragedy myself. At this point, I could tell my tank was dangerously close to empty, yet I didn't have time to refill. I was running on autopilot. Many people turned to me for strength, but I had very little to offer. My energy was gone.

"I don't know what's wrong with me," I complained to my wife, Cathy. "I've completely bottomed out, and my reserve tank is drained too."

"Now you understand how some people in your congregation feel most of the time," she gently replied.

Two weeks after the funeral, I spoke to a group of pastors in northern Minnesota. I really didn't want to go but couldn't bring myself to break the commitment.

After muddling halfheartedly through my presentations, I bid a quick farewell and headed home, hardly recognizing the autumn beauty around me.

I stopped to fill up at Kwik Trip in Brainerd, Minnesota. At the cash register, I glanced down at the newspaper stand. The front page headline blared: Mega-Church Pastor Resigns: Admits Infidelity. The man's picture accompanying the article was familiar. I had met this guy, read things he had written, and heard him speak on several occasions. He was not someone I would have suspected to have such a moral failure; but there it was, being shouted from the rooftops.

Shocked, I purchased the paper, returned to my car, and scanned the article again. As I read, the Holy Spirit spoke to me. It seemed almost audible: "This is what happens to ministers who neglect their souls."

I felt like Adam in Eden who, caught hiding, heard God's searching voice, "Where are you?" I realized I wasn't in a healthy place emotionally or spiritually.

"Oh God," I cried out, "Please don't let that ever happen to me. What can I do to take better care of my soul? I need your help. I need your strength."

The long drive home through northern tundra became a spiritual pilgrimage and my car turned into a sanctuary. In one of the sweetest seasons of prayer I've ever experienced, God revealed new truth to me and filled my heart with holy love.

I realized that I had been depending on yesterday's grace, failing to keep my spiritual life fresh and up-to-date. My soul was empty and needed to be replenished. I saw that I had been hiding behind a very busy schedule to avoid addressing significant internal issues.

On this homeward journey, I grieved the loss of my precious friends, repented of my soul's leanness, and readjusted my priorities. It took this dark night of the soul for me to discover the danger of running on empty. The commitments I made that day led to significant schedule changes and new spiritual commitments (noted in chapter 8) that have sustained me to this day.

Since then, I've made corrective adjustments regularly. It's an ongoing process, being filled anew with God's grace every morning. Occasionally, I fall short and catch myself running on an eighth of a tank again—but now I have a healthy benchmark for life alignment.

I pray that some of the things I've learned on this journey will help you in your daily quest to love and serve the Lord.

## Take a Fresh Dip

A pastor's job can be summed up in four words: *preach, pray, lead,* and *love* (not necessarily in that order). Every ministerial task is included on that short list. One thing is certain: The only way to effectively accomplish these priorities is through the fullness of Christ's Spirit. Otherwise, we are merely resounding gongs and clanging cymbals (1 Cor. 13:1).

Empty pastors are clouds without water, performing empty ministry.

Their sermons are empty.

Their prayers are empty.

Their leadership is empty.

Their relationships are empty.

The great nineteenth-century pastor, Dr. C. I. Scofield, went to church with a Welsh friend, where they heard an empty sermon on Naaman's healing as he dipped himself in the Jordan: "It was a good sermon from a homiletical standpoint, and I admitted it to myself in a kind of protest against an inner feeling that somehow, good as it was, it was leaving me cold. Just then, my friend leaned over and sighed, 'If only the dear brother would take a fresh dip in the Jordan himself!'"[1]

Have you been busy running the church, preaching empty sermons, leading empty meetings, saying empty prayers, and engaging in empty conversations? Perhaps you need to stop running, and take a fresh dip in the Jordan.

## High Calling, Hard Work

Pastoral ministry is a high and noble calling. There is no greater privilege than helping others find faith, strength, and comfort in Christ. Rightly understood, ministry is joining Jesus in his work in the world. As Methodist theologian Thomas Oden noted, "Ministry in the Christian community is a participation in the ministry of Christ. It is the ministry of the Father through the Son by the Spirit. It is a ministry offered to the whole church as gift and task."[2]

On good days, it feels like a delightful gift and fulfilling task. Easter Sunday for instance, is an annual highlight for pastors, as absentee parishioners return like the swallows of San Capistrano.

However there are other days when it is neither delightful nor fulfilling.

A few years ago, after the last of four exhilarating Easter worship services, I turned to my elder associate, Pastor Ben, and joyfully exclaimed, "Isn't this fabulous? I can't imagine it getting any better! Being a pastor is pure joy!"

Pastor Ben grinned wryly and replied, "Just wait until tomorrow."

Sure enough, Monday was another story. Pastoral counselor Arch Hart calls Monday "adrenaline letdown day." Mark Driscoll talks about "bread truck Mondays," when the fantasy of delivering bread is far more appealing than continuing in the pastorate.

That Easter Monday, problems sprang up everywhere. I had to deal with a leadership squabble, a budget challenge, a marriage crisis, and a swarm of other difficulties.

I called Pastor Ben. "This is absolutely horrible! I can't imagine it getting any worse. Being a pastor is pure torture!" He grinned and replied, "Just wait until tomorrow."

## Grace in the Grinder

Pastoral work, though rewarding, is quite difficult. Between glory moments, we're in the grinder, and the pressures are absolutely enormous. Focus on the Family reported that "45.5 percent of pastors say they've experienced depression or burnout to the extent that they needed to take a leave of absence from ministry."[3]

Leadership guru Peter Drucker stated that the four most difficult jobs in America today are: president of the United States, university president, hospital administrator, and pastor of a local church.[4] Being included on Drucker's short list somehow gives me a morose sense of satisfaction. At least somebody recognizes the difficulty of our mission.

Only those who share the pastoral load (and those married to them) comprehend the toll it takes. Yet despite the daily challenges, significant joys and fulfillment are readily available to pastors of local churches. We really can "serve the LORD with gladness" (Ps. 100:2 KJV) and "count it all joy" (James 1:2 KJV) if we are willing to take a fresh dip in the Jordan.

The only way to accomplish God's bidding is through his anointing. This is our source of strength. The most frustrating task in the world is attempting to accomplish holy work through the power of the flesh. It cannot be done. Human effort alone is merely chasing the wind (Eccl. 1:14).

## Why Do Pastors Run Empty?

Overworked, overburdened, and overstressed pastors are prone to depletion due to the involvement, investment, and intensity of the task. Burnout, or "anorexia of the soul" as Harvey Herman puts it, is a state of emotional and spiritual exhaustion.[5] In this empty condition, ministers feel drained and used up. There's little energy to deal with people. As a result, burned out pastors seek ways to escape and detach from those they serve.

How does this occur? We don't launch zombies into ministry. At ordination, when they are given authority to preach the Word and administer the sacraments, fledgling pastors embrace it eagerly, confident enough to beat hell with a water pistol. What happens? How do pastors end up dried, drained, and depleted?

### Responsibilities Exceed Energy

Ministry is always unfinished. Recently, a friend said, "It's not the pastoral work that does me in, but all the work that is left undone after the work is done."

Ministers, normally a responsible lot, desire to successfully fulfill all the duties placed upon them. The problem is that there are many more responsibilities than any human being could possibly meet.

Ministry is multitasking while solo-purposing. Seminary doesn't always prepare us well for that. Juggling a thousand issues and interactions clouds the bigger picture. After a busy season of dealing with trifles, I taped the following note on my office wall: "Why are we doing this?"

The next morning, upon entering my office, I noticed our custodian had scrawled a little response on the bottom of the page: "I have no idea and was wondering the same thing myself."

The secret to sustained, fruitful ministry is found in following the path of responsiveness rather than mere responsibility. Our goal, in the face of multiple demands, should be to respond to the Holy Spirit's promptings, bringing Christ's grace to each situation as he leads. His yoke is easy and his burden is light (Matt. 11:30). Surrounded by responsibilities, we must listen carefully for one voice—that of our Shepherd (John 10:4). It's the only voice that counts.

### Pretentions Exceed Realities

The temptation to fake it in ministry is powerful. Pastors are inclined to pretend to be more holy, prayerful, loving, and wise than they really are. Occasionally, doting parishioners place us on the holier-than-thou pedestal. Unfortunately, there's only one direction to go from there.

While counseling a young couple, I attempted to connect with the unbelieving husband by saying, "I'm a regular, ordinary guy too." The wife, obviously disappointed in my fall from superhero status, shook her head and sighed, "That's so sad, Pastor. I'll be praying for you." So far, her prayers haven't availed much. I still don't wear a cape and can't leap buildings in a single bound.

Pretention is like driving a misaligned car that always veers to the left. It takes constant effort to stay on course. As soon as you relax and loosen the grip, you end up swerving. You can fake it for a while, but sooner or later, the other you comes out and takes over. Keeping your life and ministry going the right direction is difficult when your inner life is out of line. Instead of pretending that everything is straight while struggling with the steering, why not just go to the master mechanic for a soul alignment?

## Pleasing Exceeds Shepherding

The church is fertile soil for codependency. If you need to be needed, you'll find plenty of opportunities in the ministry. In fact, the evangelical world normally rewards such neuroses. That approach, however, is dry rot to the soul. When our identity comes from others, we cease to be authentic, and end up in a never-ending quest to please. As Craig Groeschel noted, "Becoming obsessed with what people think about me is the quickest way to forget what God thinks about me."[6] In my early ministry, I fell into this trap because I tied my worth to the opinions of others. I'll never forget the day God began to free me from the dreadful disease of people pleasing.

I had promised my kids that we would enjoy a popcorn and movie night together, but while the corn was popping, the phone rang. An unhappy parishioner was on the line. "Pastor, my husband and I are upset about a few things at church. We're considering leaving, and we want you to come over to our house tonight so we can discuss the problems."

Codependent Mark kicked in. I gulped and said, "Of course, I'll be there right away." Hanging up, I turned to face my five children staring at me in wide-eyed dismay.

"Dad! Where are you going? Why are you doing that? What about the popcorn and movies?"

At that moment, the clue phone rang for Mr. Wilson, and for the first time I saw myself as a rotten, twisted, people pleaser.

"Kids, you're right," I declared. "I made a promise to you and, doggone it, I'm going to keep it."

I took a deep breath, grabbed the phone before losing confidence, and called the lady back. With the rest of the family eavesdropping, I informed her that I couldn't come that night after all because I had already made a promise to have popcorn and movies with my kids, and I needed to keep it. She didn't understand and tried to pressure me, but I held my ground and found tremendous joy and liberty as the approval addiction chains fell away.

My family cheered when I hung up, and the popcorn was the tastiest I'd ever had. I lost a disgruntled couple from my church that night but gained my soul and kept my kids. Looking back, over a decade later, I think it was a fantastic trade.

### Outflow Exceeds Inflow

There is a continual ebb and flow in ministry. Even when things are going right, we need repeated infillings for our outflowings. There's no other way for effective, vibrant, long-term ministry. "The more you experience God's power working in your life and through your ministry," said Wesley Duewel, "the more you will sense your repeated need of the Spirit's new touch."[7] Pouring our lives out for others without taking the necessary steps to replenish leads to ministry fatigue, much like the experience I related at the beginning of this chapter.

Pastor, the *best* gift you can give your people is your own healthy soul and your heart overflowing with God's holy love. You can't give them that unless you take the time to nourish your soul.

"Beloved," said A. B. Simpson, "Let us drink of the living waters. Nay, let us receive them into our very hearts, so that we shall carry the fountain with us wherever we go."[8]

Sadly, too many pastors are so busy running the church that they don't take time to run to Jesus. Several years ago, my seminary professor, C. Peter Wagner, conducted a survey of 572 pastors across America about their prayer lives. He discovered that the pastors spent an average of twenty-two minutes a day in prayer, with 57 percent reporting less than twenty minutes.[9]

No wonder so many ministers are fatigued, frazzled, and frayed. It's impossible to meet the overwhelming demands of ministry on less than twenty minutes a day. That's like eating only one small carrot in the morning and expecting it to nourish you all day long.

## Serving Exceeds Loving

You serve God, but do you love him? You work hard for him, but do you enjoy him? After all, according to the Westminster Catechism, the chief end of man is to glorify God and to enjoy him forever.

You serve your congregation, but do you love them? You work with people, but do you enjoy them? I think there should be a pastors' catechism that calls us to love our people and enjoy them forever.

A rookie pastor, at lunch with a seasoned ministry veteran, unburdened his heart, complaining about his congregation nonstop for an hour and a half. At the end of the conversation, the older pastor looked the young man squarely in the eye and said, "I know exactly what will solve these problems."

"What? Please, tell me," the young pastor responded.

"You must learn to love your people. You are serving them out of duty, but you don't love them much and they can feel it. You need to go home, get alone with God, and beg him to place a new love in your heart for your flock. If you do that, you will be amazed at how many of these challenges will be resolved."

One day, swamped with difficulties, I called my mentor, Loring Peterson. "I need your help," I implored. "I have problems on every side here at the church, and I need you to pray for the Lord to take them away."

I was shocked by Loring's blunt answer: "No."

"N-No?" I stammered. "I thought you cared about me."

"I do," Loring replied. "That's why I won't ask God to take away your problems. I'm assuming that all those problems have to do with people, and if God took all the problems, he'd have to take all people too. You don't want *that* do you?"

"Well, of course not," I said, then thought for a minute and added, "But can I pick just a few?"

In essence, ministry is loving God, loving others, and helping others love God. Neil Cole observed, "The Gospel flies best on the wings of relationships."[10]

In an effort to do this, we need to wait on the Lord. There are two distinct ways to do this: the Martha method and the Mary method.

When Jesus came to their house, Martha waited like a busy waitress, stressed out, and scurrying around in manic mode. Mary waited on him in a completely different fashion. She simply sat at Jesus' feet, waiting to hear what he had to say. Jesus said she chose the better way. Martha was so busy serving that she didn't have time for loving. I frequently find myself acting like Martha, flailing away and imagining I'm doing something great for God, when all he wants from me is to wait at his feet and listen to what he has to say. In the words of Corrie ten Boom, "Don't wrestle, just nestle."[11] An African adage puts it another way: "There will be such sweet reward when we wait upon the Lord."[12]

## Duty Exceeds Delight

In his beautiful book *The Return of the Prodigal Son*, Henri Nouwen wrote, "I have become accustomed to living with sadness, and so have lost the eyes to see my joy."[13]

When we lose our eyes to see the joy, everything grows dim. Troubles are what you see when you take your eyes off Jesus.

I live in snow country, and after it sticks in November, people here don't see the ground again until April. One cold December morning, I looked out our picture window upon fourteen inches that had fallen overnight. "Arrgh!" I complained. "Fourteen inches of obligation." When my kids woke up, they looked out the same window, shouted, "Yippee!" and ran to put on snow clothes. For them, it was fourteen inches of opportunity. Same snow—different perspective.

Ministry is obligation or opportunity, depending on how you approach it. The more love you put into it and the more time you take for soul refreshment, the more it will be delightful rather than burdensome.

## The Deeper Root

What drives ministers to overwork, assume too much responsibility, and serve out of grim duty? We realize there's a better way but frequently fail to reflect this understanding as we approach the work.

I believe this vain striving is rooted in another issue. We are trying to prove our worth, compensating for a deep inner wound caused by unmet needs, unhealed hurts, and unfulfilled expectations.

A hole in the soul compels us to meet our need for acceptance and affirmation by working hard and overloading with responsibilities. We try to assuage our pain by pretending and people pleasing. We deceive ourselves into thinking that we can meet unrealistic, unfulfilled expectations by hard work and dutiful service.

None of this works.

## The Solution at the Center

The answer lies in Christ alone at the spiritual center where, as Quaker Thomas Kelley said, "The breath and stillness of Eternity are upon us."[14]

### For Unmet Needs, Jesus Is the Answer

Philippians 4:19 says, "My God will meet all your needs according to his glorious riches in Christ Jesus." Jehovah Jireh—the Lord is my provider.

### For Unhealed Hurts, Jesus Is the Answer

Malachi 4:2 says, "But for you who revere my name, the sun of righteousness will rise with healing in its wings. And you will go out and leap like calves released from the stall." Jehovah Rapha—the Lord is my healer.

### For Unfilled Expectations, Jesus Is the Answer

Second Thessalonians 2:16–17 says, "May our Lord Jesus Christ himself and God our Father, who loved us and by his grace gave us eternal encouragement and good hope, encourage your hearts and strengthen you in every good deed and word." Jehovah Shammah—the Lord who is there. El Shaddai—God Almighty.

## Like a Donut

A child's song says, "Life without Jesus is like a donut, because there's a hole in the middle of your heart."[15] The same goes for ministry. It's like a donut: there's a hole in the middle of everything you do, say, organize, preach, and teach unless Jesus is in the center.

As ministers, we're constantly drawn to focus on people, and this is pleasing to Christ. After all, he said, "Whatever you did for one of the least of these brothers of mine, you did for me" (Matt. 25:40). But as we focus on others, let us never forget to be centered on Christ—for he is the answer for our life, ministry, and people.

> My people have committed two sins: They have forsaken me,
> the spring of living water, and have dug their own cisterns,
> broken cisterns that cannot hold water.
>
> —Jeremiah 2:13

# 2
# Broken Cisterns
## Empty Churches

### Larry Who?

Pancreatic cancer. Six months to live. The doctor's words echoed in Larry Bingham's mind as he tried to come to grips with the stark diagnosis. Retiring from the post office only three months earlier, he planned to fish and travel to Europe with his wife, Pam. But now, everything had changed.

They drove home in a long silence.

Finally, Pam spoke. "Honey, I think we need to start going to church," For once, Larry didn't object. Maybe the man upstairs could help him through this ordeal.

The next Sunday, Larry and Pam dressed up and drove to the little white church on the corner. When they walked into the foyer, a half-hearted usher grunted an awkward greeting and handed them a bulletin.

Upon entering the sanctuary, the Binghams immediately felt tension in the air. About fifty people gathered for worship that morning, and they all seemed distracted and discouraged. Larry and Pam knew nothing about the difficult board meeting the previous week or the recent conflict resulting in two families leaving the church. All they knew was that this place made them feel very uncomfortable.

The preacher rambled through a semi-prepared sermon that he had downloaded from the Internet on Saturday night, and concluded with a long, droning prayer. Nobody spoke to the Binghams as they quickly exited, but they didn't mind. They had already decided to never return.

"Let them keep their lame religion," Larry commented on the drive home. "It doesn't do anything for me. We'll do just fine without it."

When Larry died seven months later, the funeral director called the pastor of the little white church on the corner, asking if he would conduct the funeral.

"Larry who?" Pastor Jones replied. "I'm sorry, but I can't say I ever met the man."

## Do We Have Something to Offer?

Larry Bingham lives in your community. Maybe he and his wife will attend your church this weekend. Perhaps they showed up last Sunday. If they were in your worship service last week, what did they experience? Did they sense the powerful presence of God? Did they receive real spiritual help?

In times of need, thirsty people turn to the church for streams of life-giving water. Too often, they find a broken cistern instead.

Within the shadow of the steeple, our neighbors search for answers to life's perplexing questions. Do we have anything to give them?

With family fractures, economic upheaval, and social injustices abounding, the world wonders how to make sense of life that is unraveling. Is there any meaning in all of this?

Hunger for spiritual things is deepening. Several of Amazon's top twenty best sellers deal with spiritual themes. However, most of the spirituality found in those pages is not from a biblical perspective. Thirsty people gulp down whatever they can find. They're drinking spiritual salt water that never satisfies and only leads to greater thirst. Shouldn't Christ's church provide them with something better?

## The Great Disappointment

The church was created to be the spring of spiritual vitality for the neighbors and nations. Sadly, in recent years the world has looked to the church only to discover a church looking to the world for answers. Instead of giving hope, we've settled for a tepid and uninspiring religiosity—the bland leading the bland. "So, because you are lukewarm—neither hot nor cold—I am about to spit you out of my mouth" (Rev. 3:16).

The church has fallen into a sorry state of lukewarm disrepair. Rather than counteracting the growing ungodliness in our culture, we have capitulated to the spirit of this age. Some congregations, reacting to society's alarming trends, hunker down in holy huddles that provide neither salt nor light. Instead of reaching out to lost and broken people, they're hiding from them or even fighting with them. God forgive us. Something must change.

It takes life to bring forth life. Dead churches aren't going to have babies. Dead Christians aren't going to win lost souls. Broken cisterns aren't going to produce living water. We need to come alive if we expect to share life.

Shortly before an old pastor died, he wrote the following poem to be read at his funeral: "Tell my congregation, as they cry and shed wild tears, that I am no more dead right now than they have been for years."[1]

## Empty Churches

Lifeless churches are empty, and the emptiness comes in two forms: anemic and artificial.

### Anemic Church: Obvious Emptiness

Often, the emptiness is obvious because nobody is sitting in the pews. Declining churches cherish faded memories of former glory days. A low-grade dissatisfaction, mingled with lethal complacency, leads to a downward spiral that is nearly impossible to correct.

Leaders scratch their heads, wondering why the neighbors are disinterested. It's time for a reality check. Who wants to join something that's not going anywhere? Who wants to drink from a broken cistern?

Please understand that I am not speaking against small churches. Countless small, vibrant, life-giving congregations are truly on mission. They care consistently, live passionately, believe boldly, and demonstrate faithfulness continually. Certainly, these churches are alive and thriving regardless of their size. A church's vitality is not measured by how many people fill the pews, but rather by how much those people are filled with Jesus.

However, the spiritual drought around us is obvious. In fallow seasons of dryness, churches that once reached out to the community are now barely holding on for survival. Worship services are routinely boring. Ministries decline as the membership ages without any infusion of new, younger families. The primary discussion at board meetings is about keeping certain people happy and the doors open.

### Artificial Church: Faking Fullness

On the opposite side of the spectrum are congregations that appear to be thriving, when in reality they too are spiritually empty. Like the Sardis church in Revelation, they "have a reputation of being alive, but [they] are dead" (3:1).

Churches may have multitudes in the pews and plenty of programs but may also still be broken cisterns, void of God's life-giving presence.

How does this happen?

## Full of Other Things

Empty churches, both anemic and artificial, are that way because they're filled with lesser things.

### Power Struggles

Too often, life is squeezed out of a church by a power struggle. One or two long-tenured families feel entitled to call the shots, preventing new initiatives from gaining traction. Their theme song is "I Shall Not Be Moved!"

In the order of Diotrephes, who "likes to put himself first" (3 John 9 ESV), power-hungry people sabotage progress by undermining leadership and resisting necessary changes.

Sometimes, the fault lies with an immature, unwise, or uncaring pastor who attempts to drive people rather than shepherd them. When shepherds fail to lead with love, the sheep balk and bite.

Several years ago, at a Wilson family reunion, the food wasn't ready yet and my three-year-old son had a meltdown. His uncle Tim grinned and said, "That little fellow is cranky 'cause he's so hungry." Then he looked at me and shared this profound insight, "You know, when church people ain't gettin' fed, they get cranky too."

Through ignorance, arrogance, or neglect, a pastor may largely bear the responsibility for crankiness in the congregation. However, innumerable churches have a long history of good-hearted, short-tenured pastorates, while entrenched power brokers remain unchanged.

## Petty Strife

In the absence of vision, pettiness prevails. When conversations turn to bickering and backbiting—rather than growing in grace, blessing the neighbors, and transforming the community—something is terribly awry. The grieved Holy Spirit will cease flowing in a church where unhealthy strife and dissensions abound.

"Mine!" "Give it back!" WHAP! "I'm telling Mo-oooom!" Oh, the blissful words of children at play. Whenever there's an interaction like that, I can guarantee you: somebody is being selfish.

Grown-ups act that way too. A person might be sixty years old and still prone to temper tantrums. "Mine! I want my way or else!" WHAP! When fur flies in the squabble, I can guarantee you: somebody is being selfish.

The reflective monk Thomas Merton said, "To consider persons and events and situations only in the light of their effect upon myself is to live on the doorstep of hell."[2] Self-centeredness is the root of most conflict. Show me a church full of strife and I'll guarantee you: somebody is being selfish.

Children of Christian leaders are often the sad casualties of squabbling and nitpicking. The discord they witness while growing up sours them on church participation. Some walk away from the faith altogether, echoing Gandhi's reputed sentiment, "I'd be a Christian if it weren't for the Christians."

## Self-Pity

When a congregation struggles for survival, its members often suffer from corporate low self-esteem: "People like to join a good church. Nobody is joining us. Therefore, we're not a good church."

A rural church member once met me in the musty basement nursery room. We sat in little toddler-size plastic chairs as he unburdened his heart, weeping. "What's wrong with us?"

He was asking the right question. "What's wrong with us?" is a perfect catalyst, if you move toward positive change. Otherwise, it's just a gloomy invitation to a pity party. There are four problems with pity parties.

**There Is No Music.** There is no praise and thanksgiving for what the Lord has done. Nobody brings a banjo or accordion. Nobody dances or sings, except for perhaps a mournful rendition of the blues.

**There Are No Refreshments.** There is no thriving communion with God and fellowship with other believers. Nobody serves cream puffs at a pity party. There's nothing refreshing about it. The only thing dished up is a stew of rehashed offenses and complaints.

**There Are No Guests.** Send out the invitation and no one shows up.

**There Is No Hope.** Hopelessness is what fuels the party and keeps it going. Consumed with self-pity, a brighter future seems unattainable.

## Busy Activity

Isaiah 28:10 speaks to over-committed, duty bound, religious people: "For it is: Do and do, do and do, rule on rule, rule on rule; a little here, a little there." Sometimes, churches can be so caught up in the *doing* that they fail to *be* God's people. There's a reason we're called human beings rather than human doings. Who we are is far more important than what we do.

Be careful not to be so busy doing great things for God that you neglect the greater thing. It's possible to put together an entire worship service without truly worshiping the Creator. Programming, budgeting, visioning, leading, and planning—though important— are all empty without the empowering presence of the Holy Spirit. Never let working for God substitute for his glorious work in you.

## Popular Appeasement

An inordinate desire for approval leads to worldly compromise, muting the challenging points of discipleship and holiness. Although it's imperative to reach out and love everyone, we must not change our message to accommodate sinful patterns and perspectives.

When the winds of culture shift, it's tempting for churches to sail along with breezes of popular opinion. This is why God's Word is our dependable anchor. It keeps us tethered to truth. Regardless of how the wind blows or what society thinks, we must stand firmly on biblical ground.

When we reinterpret the Bible to make it say what we wish it said, we end up playing games and straddling fences. Fence straddlers are "mug-wumps"—with the mug on one side and the wump on the other—never taking a stand and merely reflecting a worldly culture rather than transforming it. Church, void of biblical conviction, is like cotton candy: delightful for a moment, but lacking substance, quickly melts away.

## The Relentless Quest for Cool

Church leaders often attend conferences, read books, and follow blogs hoping for a fresh dose of coolness to spice things up a bit. Entrepreneurs make a lot of money creating and selling the newest, coolest ministry fads to hapless pastors who often follow like lemmings.

Now, I thank God for my ministerial friends who have been endowed with an extraordinary measure of coolness. Like any other gift, they should use it to glorify God and expand his kingdom. If you're cool, be cool for Jesus!

However, church leaders consumed with being cool quickly lose their heat. You can't be hot when you're trying too hard to be cool. Such efforts easily backfire, and even repel the very people we're trying to attract.

The pressing concern isn't what kind of music you have in your worship services or whether you use the latest technology. It's not a matter of edgy programming or awesome events. It is, instead, an issue of the heart. Are you sold out for God? Are you full of Jesus? Is holy fire burning in your belly? Are you passionate about spiritual things? Are you 100 percent surrendered? Do you love God fervently?

The coolest ministry initiatives in the world won't meet the most significant spiritual need in our congregations and communities. Broken and needy people, like Larry Bingham, aren't looking for cool church programs. They are searching for genuine love and spiritual wholeness. This comes only through prayer and the power of the Holy Spirit.

# Relevant Revival

We need renewal! We need a fresh outpouring of holy love and divine power—a relevant revival. It's time for stale churches to freshen up and for shallow churches to go deep.

A while back, I received two invitations to pastors' conferences on the same day. The theme of the first conference was relevance. There was an inspiring slate of innovative pastors who live on the cutting edge. They guaranteed the silver bullet for only 249 dollars, if you sign up for the early bird special. Something about it rang hollow—felt too much like the quest for cool.

The second conference, with a revival theme, was easier on the wallet. I was impressed by the meaty seminars: prayer, stewardship, and holiness. Yet, somehow, it felt stale—like these folks were out of touch, lagging twenty or thirty years behind in cultural understanding and communication.

I wondered, is it possible to blend those two perspectives into one? Can we be people of prayer and holiness, missional ministry, and cultural relevance? Is it possible to passionately pursue the fullness of God and community transformation? Does fervent prayer belong only to the older women? Is revival only for fire-breathing fundamentalists in business suits? Is there a new way to experience the old time religion?

I did a blog search the other day on the words *relevance* and *revival*. I discovered that few younger, missional bloggers ever use the word *revival*, but they use *relevance* repeatedly. On the other hand, the negative discernment bloggers (who suffer from what B. T. Roberts called "a warring holiness") use *revival* often, in the sense that they are longing for, but not experiencing it. They also use *relevance* occasionally, always viewing it as something to be avoided at all costs.

Both the emerging missional and the discernment bloggers are missing something. We need revival in our hearts, homes, and churches for any hope of healing in our land. The challenge before us is not primarily a social concern. Social transformation comes through personal renewal. Our churches desperately need revival. On the other hand, revival needs to be relevant. If we're filled and fired up for God but can't communicate this reality effectively with the rising generation, we will fizzle. The blessing is for sharing. If we don't share it clearly and compellingly, then they won't believe or experience it.

I'm a student of revival movements in history. "Revival," said Leonard Ravenhill, "is when God gets so sick and tired of being misrepresented that He shows Himself."[3]

In my research, I have discovered that every time God moves mightily across a land he sets his people to praying. There is always a call to re-dig the old wells of repentance, faith, holiness, and scriptural obedience. Also, this message is delivered in a brand new way. In every movement, God brings his ancient truth with a fresh, new communication. True revival is always relevant because God shows up, pouring holy love into our hearts that flows outward to others. That's as relevant and real as it gets.

## Larry Bingham Remix

What would have happened to Larry and Pam Bingham if the little white church on the corner had been filled with Christ's loving presence rather than all the other junk?

Two weeks before Larry received the devastating medical report, Pastor Jones did some soul searching. In an extended time of prayer, God revealed that he had been running on empty, trying to accomplish God's work in the power of the flesh. He prayed for a fresh outpouring of the Holy Spirit, and the Lord powerfully answered with a new anointing of joy.

The board meeting was bathed in prayer, and the pastor shared his recent spiritual renewal. Although not every decision was unanimous, the unity of the Spirit prevailed.

Pastor Jones contacted the two departed families, humbly seeking forgiveness for the hurtful things that had been said. Both expressed their pardon and appreciation for the call. The next Sunday, one of the families came back.

On Saturday night as Pastor Jones prayed over his sermon, God revealed fresh insights beyond what he had originally prepared. He followed the divine nudge and adjusted the sermon.

The next morning, the pastor showed up early to pray, and then greeted the parishioners joyfully as they arrived for the worship service. Soon, the whole church was abuzz with animated conversation. Two strangers came in, and several of the members introduced themselves to Larry and Pam Bingham.

At the conclusion of the message, Pastor Jones invited anyone who needed special prayer to come forward. Larry and Pam nervously made their way to the front of the church, where several members of the congregation gathered around them in loving support.

Seven months later, Larry's funeral was held at the little white church on the corner. As Pam departed, she hugged Pastor Jones and his wife, saying, "I'm so glad we met you people! You are like family. Thank you for taking us into your hearts and homes. Larry found his peace with God because of you. I can't tell you how much that means to me today."

Now, *that* is relevant revival!

> Who may ascend the hill of the LORD? Who may stand in his holy place? He who has clean hands and a pure heart, who does not lift up his soul to an idol or swear by what is false.
>
> —Psalm 24:3–4

# 3

# Catharsis
## Empty Out to Fill Up

Empty churches. Empty Christians. Empty pastors. Empty hearts. All share something in common. They desperately need filling but are already too full. We can't be filled with the Holy Spirit when we're bloated with other things.

## Can't Take the Turkey

A newlywed couple took the long drive home for a 4:00 p.m. Thanksgiving dinner. The bride's mother worked feverishly in the kitchen, creating a feast bigger than Belshazzar's. She eagerly anticipated the banquet especially prepared for her daughter and new son-in-law.

In his rush to hit the road, the young husband failed to eat breakfast. Hunger pangs kicked in around noon, but he fought them valiantly. By 2:00 p.m., however, he was famished and could stand it no longer. He swung into a market for a little bite. He purchased a box of Milk Duds, two Snickers, and three donuts, wolfing them down in under four minutes.

Two hours later, at his in-laws' candlelit dinner table, he was unable to eat. His belly was so full of junk food that he couldn't take the turkey.

Spiritually, like that foolish young man, we cram ourselves with junk and lose our appetite for greater things. We can't take the turkey because we're already too full.

## Confessing and Repenting

We must empty out before we can fill up. We will not enjoy Christ's fullness until we first experience the emptiness. We cannot receive wholeness without brokenness, or victory without humility. Obedience brings the blessing. This is a call to honest confession and genuine repentance.

For many years, I figured confessing and repenting were for "those people"—unconverted pagans—and not for fairly faithful religious folks like me. However, self-righteousness, haughtiness, hypocrisy, and gossip are certainly conditions that need confessing and repenting. And all those behaviors are rife within churches.

There will never be a relevant revival in our land unless Christians, starting with the leaders, confess, repent of, and renounce their sin. It begins with us—the household of faith.

When asked how revival comes about, the great English evangelist Gypsy Smith responded, "Go home, lock yourself in your room, kneel down in the middle of the floor. Draw a chalk mark all around yourself and ask God to start the revival inside that chalk mark. When He has answered your prayer, the revival will be on."[1]

Confession means "one word" with Christ. When I confess Christ, I declare that my life is one word with his. Whatever he says, I say it too. Whatever he wants, I want it too. We all need to confess.

Repentance means "to turn or change." If I'm off course, even just a tiny little bit, I must turn and make the necessary corrections to align my life with Christ. Wherever he leads, I'll follow. Whatever he asks, I'll do.

It would serve us well to heed Peter's message from Acts 3:19: "Repent, then, and turn to God so that your sins may be wiped out, that times of refreshing may come from the Lord." We all need to repent.

## Sin Management

Willful sin is the first place to start emptying. We must declare war on any action, thought, attitude, word, or habit that displeases the Lord.

Without conscious effort, we easily slide into the sin management business, harboring and justifying pet sins, rather than confessing and repenting of them. The result is a sinning religion—a state of spiritual disobedience—that looks a whole lot more like the world, the flesh, and the devil than like Jesus.[2] The consuming concern of sin management is: "How much sinning can I get away with?" That's the wrong question.

A wealthy lady interviewed three men for a chauffeur position. "How close can you get to the edge of a cliff without falling off?"

she asked. The first guy said, "Twelve inches." The second guy said, "Six inches." The third guy said, "I'll stay as far from the cliff as I can." He got the job.

When staying close to the cliff appeals more to us than staying close to Christ, we are trying to manage sin. Spiritual victory is never found along the fuzzy edges of compromise. God calls us to steer clear of the cliff altogether.

Holding on to cherished sins is like keeping pet rattlesnakes in your closet. Sooner or later, you're going to get bitten. Careless, compromising Christianity is a false substitute for the real thing. "Shall we continue in sin that grace may abound? Certainly not!" (Rom. 6:1–2 NKJV).

Empty the obvious! Refuse to make excuses for sinning. You might say, "That's just the way I am." But is it Christ's best for you? Weren't you created to live above that? Some say, "Follow your heart." The tricky part is that hearts are deceitful (Jer. 17:9).

I once confronted a confused young man who left his wife for another woman. I said he was sinning and needed to get right with God. "No, no!" he protested. "That's not true. I prayed about it, and God told me it's alright."

The poor dude must have been praying to another deity—perhaps the false idol of self-indulgence. He was following his heart, but he certainly wasn't hearing from heaven on that one.

Satan, the deceiver, lures us into falsely assuming it must be true if it feels right. We delude ourselves into thinking that wrong is not so bad in this particular instance. Deep down we still know right from wrong. Justifying bad behavior never justifies us before almighty God. Scripture clearly calls us to renounce our sins rather than excuse them.

## Spider Webs and Rust Spots

If we only battle outward sin, we will merely experience outward righteousness.[3] Spiritual cleansing goes far deeper than that. It means going after the spider instead of just sweeping its webs.

We need to address the sin (singular) that resides deep in the heart, which leads to sins (plural). This sin condition has various labels: iniquity, the sinful nature, the old man, the flesh, and carnality; but it all comes back to one thing—an inner contrariness toward the deeper things of God. It is the well of wrong-being from which all wrongdoing springs. As Henry David Thoreau noted, "There are a thousand hacking at the branches of evil to one who is striking at the root."[4]

I've been dealing with rust spots on the back door for several years. Each summer the rust shows up, so I dab white paint over it. By midwinter, the rust spots pop up again. Slapping on a coat of paint won't really fix the problem. The corrosion will continue until I deal with it at a deeper level. Isn't that the way it works spiritually?

Transformation occurs when we completely open ourselves to the Great Physician, allowing him to conduct extensive soul surgery. This requires courageous vulnerability.

John Newton captured this thought in the following hymn, "I Asked the Lord That I Might Grow":

I asked the Lord that I might grow
In faith, and love, and every grace;
Might more of His salvation know,
And seek, more earnestly, His face.

Instead of this, He made me feel
The hidden evils of my heart;
And let the angry pow'rs of hell
Assault my soul in every part.

Lord, why is this, I trembling cried,
Wilt thou pursue thy worm to death?
"Tis in this way," the Lord replied,
I answer prayer for grace and faith

These inward trials I employ,
From self, and pride, to set thee free;
And break thy schemes of earthly joy,
That thou may'st find thy all in Me.[5]

If we're honest with God, and allow him free access to our hearts, he will come in and conduct a total cleaning. "Make no pretensions before God, but lay bare your soul," said Charles Spurgeon. "Let him see it as it is, and then he will be faithful and just to forgive you your sins and to cleanse you from all unrighteousness."[6]

## Hidden Transgressions

Some sins are obvious and blatant. We recognize and struggle with them. Others are more subtle, and we fail to notice them in ourselves.

A red-faced parishioner accosted me after church one Sunday. "Pastor, you need to preach more against sin." So, I did. The next Sunday, I preached against three whitewashed sins of the church:

gossip, greed, and gluttony. Exiting, he shook my hand and muttered, "I didn't mean *those* sins!"

It's much easier to point out others' faults than to admit our own, especially when it comes to sins of attitude.

Waging war on sin uncovers the clandestine terrorists lurking in our hearts. Taking "captive every thought" is our battle cry (2 Cor. 10:5). What inner fugitives must be apprehended before you experience spiritual fullness?

## Desire to Control

One symptom of our fallen nature is the tendency to try to control circumstances, outcomes, and other people. The bent toward controlling is a manifestation of mistrust, as we assume God's responsibility upon ourselves. This is a nuanced form of idolatry.

Seasoned saints who would never imagine committing vile, outward sin will nevertheless sin in the heart by this habit of over-controlling. It's a quality control issue really. Sooner or later, we all have to face this question: Do I want quality in my life, or do I want control? We can't have both. When we're trying to control everything and everybody around us, the quality automatically declines.

Thus, those who follow the path of perfectionism aim for a quality outcome, but end up with the exact opposite. You can't control your way to quality.

The only thing the Bible tells us to control is ourselves. And self-control is a fruit produced only by the Holy Spirit (Gal. 5:23). This is a matter of self-surrender rather than self-effort.

What (or who) have you been trying to control lately? How would it be different if you viewed the situation with complete trust and holy abandonment?

## Selfish Ambition

Success-oriented individuals are often hindered spiritually by selfish ambition. The desire to achieve and get ahead replaces a longing for Christlikeness. Wesley called this "the immense thirst of praise."[7] Sadly, such worldly ambition is often rewarded—even in the church.

Many congregations are more concerned about nickels and noses than Christlikeness. If pastoral search committees are not filled with godly wisdom, they will choose charisma over character and talent over trustworthiness. This leads to a ministry of the flesh that may appear successful for a season, but ultimately comes to nothing.

One night, a successful pastor had a dream. An angel put all his accomplishments into a furnace to test them. When the testing was over, all that was left was a miniscule heap of gold. The angel explained that the rest had disintegrated because it was just wood, hay, and stubble.

Selfish ambition is a pile of wood, hay, and stubble which is destroyed in the fire. The only thing that counts is spiritual gold.

## Double-Mindedness

Sometimes, as John Wesley said, it is possible to please Christ and ourselves. But there are also times when we can only please Christ by denying ourselves.[8] A divided heart wobbles.

One of the greatest frustrations pastors face is keeping unstable saints propped up. At times, being a pastor feels somewhat like being the pin setter at a bowling alley. As soon as you get one pin set up, two others fall over.

The reason for such spiritual instability is double-mindedness (James 1:8). We seek Christ and something else: popularity, wealth, acclaim, or comfort—Christ and the latest fad the world offers.

Whenever we seek the *and* after Christ, we're saying Christ is not enough. The reality is quite opposite.

Christ is enough! He is always more than enough for this life as well as the next. As the apostle Paul declared, "For to me, to live is Christ and to die is gain" (Phil. 1:21).

Several years ago, when our church was in the middle of a major construction project, I found myself filled with fear. Things weren't turning out the way I had expected. The congregation wasn't coming along with me as I felt they should. In a moment of discouragement, I picked up the phone and called Don, a retired pastor, who had navigated similar situations during his fruitful ministry. After I explained everything to him, there was a long pause. Then, Don responded, "Mark, as you shared your concerns, a picture came to my mind. I saw you walking on marbles—unsteady, slipping and sliding, this way and that. Before you can resolve the issues you've presented to me, you need to get your feet down on solid ground. You can't fight the good fight of faith when you're walking on marbles."

## Self-Absorption

As a straggling member of the baby boom tribe, I cringe when I realize how selfish we have been. Baby boomers are described as "the most self-absorbed generation in American history."[9]

Brian Mosely, president of the RightNow Campaign made the following observation: "We live in an extremely consumer-driven culture that tells us that the customer is number one. The customer is always right. I can have it my way. I deserve the best. This consumerism has crept into the church and turned church members into customers. The church exists to serve me and my family."[10]

The rising tide of consumerism has flooded the church, leaving us with membership rosters glutted with names of people who see themselves as club members rather than missionaries.

When our priorities revolve around self, we won't sacrifice much. It's simply too painful and difficult. After all, we have enough problems of our own without bothering to carry the crosses of others. Serving, then, becomes a matter of convenience rather than commitment. We gladly help as long as it fits with our agenda and makes us feel good.

When self-absorption rises to the level of church leadership, the decisions prove less than inspiring. One eye-opening exercise for church leadership teams is to create a list of everything that happens in the congregation—all the events, programs, and activities. Once that list is made, ask the question: "Who is this for?" Most churches will discover they are spending an inordinate amount of time, energy, and resources on themselves.

Spiritual emptiness results from being too consumed with our own way, work, and will. Dethroning self is the pathway to fullness. This is our Creator's great desire for us.

## Bud, Bread, and Two Tablets

I believe that's the point of the fascinating artifacts Moses placed inside the ark of the covenant: Aaron's rod, a golden jar of manna, and the stone tablets inscribed with the Ten Commandments (Heb. 9:3–9).

### The Budding Rod Represents God's Way

Aaron's budding rod was a definite miracle, demonstrating divine power and authority. God is in charge. We are not! Our job is to seek his way rather than demanding our own. Instead of me writing the check and asking God to sign it, I need to sign a blank check and ask God to write it.

## The Jar of Manna Represents God's Work

Many years ago, I learned the power of ten two-letter words: If it is to be, it is up to me. In matters of leadership, this phrase is often appropriate and helpful. Too many people sit around waiting for somebody to do something without realizing they are somebody.

However, I have discovered that sometimes that last two-letter word, *me*, gets in the way. Someone once defined *ego* as E.G.O.—Edging God Out. When I rush ahead and try to work things out my own way, I generally make a mess of it. The jar of manna reminds us that we can trust the Lord completely. He always provides our daily bread. If we are not living by faith, we are not living right. Ultimately, he is the one who speaks the ten two-letter words: If it is to be, it is up to *me*.

## The Ten Commandments Represent God's Will

The challenge before us is shaping our lives around God's design, rather than molding him into ours. Someone has observed, "God made man in his own image, and man returned the favor."[11]

We keep God in a little box, treat him like a pet, coax him to do tricks for us, and end up disappointed. God makes a very poor pet. Regardless of how we try, he remains completely untamed.[12]

## Is He Mine or Am I His?

A nine-year-old boy received a full-grown St. Bernard for Christmas. Viewing his new present with wonder, he exclaimed, "Wow! That's great! But is he mine or am I his?"

That's a wonderful question for every Christian: Is the Lord mine or am I his? The answer ought to be, "Yes!" Blessed assurance, Jesus is mine! He is my Savior, friend, deliverer, joy, and strength. But we must never forget who he is and that we can't own him.

We're his. We certainly do not have the right to order him around. Instead of telling God what to do, it's better to ask what he wants us to do.

The Ten Commandments remind us of this simple but beautiful prayer spoken at a banquet by baseball legend Bobby Richardson: "God, your will. Nothing more. Nothing less. Nothing else." God's way—not mine! God's work—not mine! God's will—not mine!

Is this your heart's desire? If so, how bad do you want it?

## How Bad Do You Want It?

A young seeker visited an old monk, asking how to live a holy life. Suddenly, the old man reached out, grabbed the young man's head, and shoved it down into a bucket of water. He held the flailing pilgrim down in the bucket for a long time. Finally, the monk let go and the guy popped up, sputtering, "Good grief! You idiot! You were trying to drown me! What was that all about? Are you insane?"

The old man replied, "When you become as desperate for holiness as you were for air just now, you find it."

"Blessed are those who hunger and thirst for righteousness, for they will be filled" (Matt. 5:6).

PART 2

# Repleo

to replenish, fill up, satisfy

I will make rivers flow on barren heights, and springs
within the valleys. I will turn the desert into pools of water,
and the parched ground into springs.

—Isaiah 41:18

You have made known to me the path of life; you will
fill me with joy in your presence, with eternal
pleasures at your right hand.

—Psalm 16:11

# 4

# Immersion

## Filled with God's Presence

## Settling for the Shallows

I reluctantly followed my buddies on a humid July afternoon toward Hubbell's pond. Someone concocted the idea that hot summer days demand a swimming hole. All the guys agreed—except me. The vote was four to one. Thus, I pedaled along, muttering invectives. I desired the cooling as much as they did, but faced a major obstacle: I didn't know how to swim, and ego prevented me from admitting it.

Arriving at Hubbell's Pond, the whole gang jumped in the deep end—except me. I just rolled up my pant legs and waded near the shore with the bullfrogs. While my buddies whooped and splashed in the deep end, I sulked in the shallows, swatting horseflies.

"Wasn't that great?" Ernie said as we biked home.

"Hrrumph," I disagreed. I didn't see anything great about it. "Swimming," I concluded, "isn't all it's cracked up to be."

## The Deep End

My aversion to swimming continued until I went to college and met Cathy, who happened to be a lifeguard at the local pool. I gained a sudden interest in aquatics because she was willing to give me free swimming lessons.

I'll never forget the day, at Cathy's prompting, when I finally mustered the courage to jump off the diving board. "Exhilarating," I exclaimed after the leap, "and sure beats hanging out with bullfrogs!"

That day, I finally understood Shakespeare:

There is a tide in the affairs of men,
Which, taken at the flood, leads on to fortune;
Omitted, all the voyage of their life
Is bound in shallows and in miseries.[1]

Swimming isn't really swimming until you go deep. And serving Jesus isn't really serving Jesus unless you're willing to leave the spiritual shallows for the depths. Faith rewards those who dive in all the way!

Settling for the shallows of church-ianity, we find ourselves mired in ankle-deep religion with ministry muck between the toes. We innately know that serving God must be richer and deeper than this, but our feeble works leave us depleted and disheartened, wondering why anybody would ever want what we possess. "There are a great many people in the world," said R. A. Torrey, "who have just enough religion to make themselves miserable."[2] I call that a "smidgen of religion," and plenty of church leaders suffer from this malady.

Joy in Jesus is found at the deep end of the pool. Dive in and embrace it fully. The hymn writer expressed it well: "O the deep, deep love of Jesus, vast, unmeasured, boundless, free! Rolling as a mighty ocean in its fullness over me!"[3]

## Christ-Likes

Think of three people who seem most like Jesus to you. What makes them shine? Why did you choose them? What quality marks their lives? My guess is that it doesn't have much to do with position or profession. Rather, you chose people who exude Christ's love. This is the essence of a saint and the calling of all Christians—especially those who serve in leadership.

*Christ* means "Anointed One"; therefore the word *Christians* means "little anointed ones." *Anointing* is another word for holy love. Rightly understood, *Christian* is not a philosophy or a world view. It is not an adjective to make books, music, and movies more palatable. It is not a political leaning, Kincaid painting, method of counseling, or default birthright. Instead, it is simply the description of a person living in the fullness of holy love. It means reflecting Christ as a "little anointed one." Too bad Christians have messed up the label. Comedian and social critic Bill Maher sardonically suggested, "If they would call themselves 'Christ-likes' instead of 'Christians,' maybe it would remind them to act like Jesus Christ."[4]

Although every genuine Christian wants to be more like Jesus, we often fall short of the ideal. Our strivings fail us. We don't become "Christ-likes" by working harder to become like Christ. Despite our best intentions, human efforts at holiness fall woefully short into stiff legalism and stuffy religion, which result in arrogance or despair, depending on perceived success or failure.

Only Christ brings Christlikeness. It is an inside job!

## Sponge-Ology

I occasionally use an old sponge to illustrate this point. Mr. Sponge is dry, crusty, and inflexible. Though made to release water, he will never accomplish this unless he takes a dip in the bucket.

Like a sponge that soaks in the water until saturated, Christ calls us to immerse ourselves in his love until his presence permeates every pore. We then serve in the overflow.

Christian ministry is not, therefore, a matter of working harder for Jesus, but allowing Jesus to do his mighty work in and through you: "Christ in you, the hope of glory" (Col. 1:27).

Sometimes, our Grinch-like hearts are two sizes too small. Christ's love barely trickles through such limited soul space. Open it up and let it flow. Put yourself in a place to "know this love that surpasses knowledge—that you may be filled to all the measure of the fullness of God" (Eph. 3:19).

## Total Immersion

This, I believe, is what John the Baptist meant when he said, "I baptize you with water, but he will baptize you with the Holy Spirit" (Mark 1:8). Without getting sidetracked by doctrinal distinction debates regarding the baptism of the Holy Spirit, I'd rather just say that we all need to be immersed, soaked, dipped, and plunged—baptized completely in Christ's Spirit of holy love, so that we are totally drenched and saturated with him.

Bible believers of every tribe have experienced this reality. Various faith traditions describe and manifest it differently, but the bottom line is still the same. All those rivers flow to the same ocean. God wants to fill his people completely with his presence.

Sometimes, it's a slow, gradual filling, like a person wading into the river, one step at a time. On other occasions, God pours out his Spirit dramatically in special holy moments and specific places.

## Thin Places

The Celts speak of "thin places" where heaven and earth are barely separated by a sheer veil. In such environments, we deeply sense God's profound presence. Of course, God is omnipresent. He is always everywhere.

Atheist Uncle Jack stopped little Bobby, who was on his way to Sunday school, mocking, "I'll give you a dollar if you can tell me where God is." To this the little kid replied, "Uncle Jack, I'll give you ten bucks if you can tell me where he ain't!" Nobody ever found a place where God ain't yet.

However, there are certain sacred locations and experiences in our pilgrimage, where heaven seems unusually near and you can almost reach out and touch the invisible. Victory Camp near Westerville, Ohio, was one of those thin places for me. The campground, now sold and turned into a housing development, still holds a tender spot in my heart. Recently, I drove there, searching for familiar landmarks, and recalled a sublime moment that occurred over thirty years before.

## God in a Thunderstorm

Late on the last night of youth camp the weather service issued a tornado warning. High winds howled. Electric lines snapped. A dozen young men hunkered in the raging darkness, lifting their hearts to heaven. Oakfield Cottage became a thin place, as the Almighty's holy presence immersed us. The entire band of high school boys fell on our faces, weeping before God, repenting of sin, and devoting ourselves completely to his service. At least four pastors came from that stormy vigil, including our college student counselor, John Ott, who has become an outstanding Wesleyan leader.

Occasionally, John and I run into each other at various functions, and joyfully reminisce about that special midnight hour when God met us in a thunderstorm.

## God in a Haystack

Something similar occurred back in 1806, when five Williams College students seeking shelter from a storm hid in a haystack, held a prayer meeting, and found their hearts immersed in holy love and missionary zeal.

This sacred moment captured the imaginations of those five young men for the rest of their lives. Within a century, the vision conceived in a haystack birthed one of history's greatest mission movements, touching untold millions around the world.[5]

A special outpouring of divine presence changes everything!

## God in the Upper Room

Isn't that the message of Acts 2? The upper room became a thin place, where, with a mighty rushing wind, the Holy Spirit gloriously filled the waiting disciples. This experience radically altered their future. The church was born. They found fresh courage, deep love, authentic community, and empowerment for ministry.

Before Acts 2, they were working for Jesus. After Acts 2, Jesus was working through them. There's a big difference. Most Christians still operate in the pre-Acts-2-working-for-Jesus stage, and there's not much joy or glory in that kind of servitude.

Paraphrasing Peter's Acts 2 sermon, "In the last days, God will drench us with his Spirit" (see Acts 2:17). We cannot manufacture this spiritual outpouring, but we certainly can prepare to receive it when it comes.

## The River Is There

Regardless of how God chooses to operate, our duty is to seek the River of Life and jump in. "You will seek me and find me," says the Lord, "when you seek me with all your heart (Jer. 29:13).

In Hemingway's short story "Big Two-Hearted River" we find these simple words: "The river was there."[6] Despite the destruction of everything surrounding it, the life-giving river continued to flow.

God's love is a mighty river, flowing freely, inviting us to come, plunge in, and explore the depths. It is limited only by our capacity to receive.

# How to Be Filled

So, how do we dive deep to experience the fullness of God's presence in life and ministry?

## Relinquishment

The only way to spiritual victory is through surrender. We conquer on our knees. We win by losing. We go up when we give up.

One Saturday afternoon, a Sunday school teacher prepared her classroom by pinning letters on the bulletin board to read: "Let

God." Overnight, somehow, the last letter fell from the board and the next morning, as the students entered the room, the message greeting them was "Let Go."

That's a splendid Sunday school lesson: Let go and let God.

Letting go means releasing. I release my right to be right, embracing Christ alone as my righteousness. I release my demand for how things should be, embracing reality as God's gracious gift. I release my resentment, bitterness, and cynicism, embracing forgiveness as my Balm of Gilead. I release my burdens, anxieties, and conflicts, embracing the peace of God which passes all understanding.

## Expectation

I once heard Dallas Willard assert, "You will never be more holy than you intend to be."[7] He sounded like John Wesley.

In "The Scripture Way of Salvation," Wesley proclaimed:

Look for it then every day, every hour, every moment! Why not this hour, this moment? Certainly you may look for it *now*, if you believe it is by faith. And by this token you may surely know whether you seek it by faith or by works. If by works, you want something to be done *first*, *before* you are sanctified. You think, I must first *be* or *do* thus or thus. Then you are seeking it by works unto this day. If you seek it by faith, you may expect it *as you are*; and if as you are, then expect it *now*. It is of importance to observe, that there is an inseparable connexion between these three points,—expect it *by faith*, expect it *as you are*, and expect it *now*! To deny one of them, is to deny them all; to allow one, is to allow them all.[8]

Are you living in such holy expectancy?

## Consecration

Whatever you lay on the altar is holy unto the Lord. The noted holiness evangelist Phoebe Palmer declared, "The altar sanctifies the gift."[9] The act of humble surrender, called consecration, is the secret to experiencing the fullness of Christ's presence. You'll find your soul when you lay down yourself.

Our human tendency, however, is to shrink back. We don't want to sacrifice ourselves and surrender everything. Of course, it's OK to consecrate some things to God—but we'd rather do it à la carte. Everything is too much.

My friend saw a bumper sticker that said, "Christians don't tell lies. They sing them." If we were more honest in our singing, we would say, "Some for Jesus, I surrender. Some for him, I freely give."

The only way to be filled with the Holy Spirit is to lay it all on the altar. Just to be sure you understand: all means *all*. All my sins, failures, and offenses—I lay them down. All my longings, desires, and dreams—I lay them down. All my hopes, ambitions, and agendas—I lay them down. All my relationships, communications, and entertainments—I lay them down. My past, present, and future—I lay them all down at the foot of the cross.

## Cleansing

Holiness, like soap, doesn't do much good until it is applied. You can keep it in a box, philosophize about it, and debate its merits, without ever getting around to using it.

Soul cleansing is like showering. If you skip a day, you'll be the only one to notice. If you skip a week, your family will notice. If you skip a month, everybody will notice. Indeed, using soap is much better than merely discussing it.

Malachi 3:2–3 likens God's purifying presence to "a launderer's soap" declaring that "he will purify the Levites" (ministers). This goes far beyond a feeble understanding of imputation, where God overlooks sin and pretends filthy hearts are clean.

"I'm just a poor sinner saved by grace" is a true statement, but doesn't go far enough. Yes, our Savior meets us where we are, and we don't have to clean up before we come to him, but he won't leave us where we are. He will wash, purify, and bring us to where we ought to be. May your prayer echo Robert McCheyne's, "Lord, make me as holy as a saved sinner can be."[10]

Grace overcomes not only sin's guilt, but also its power. Saving grace is keeping grace.

## Obedience

Your level of spiritual victory will never rise higher than your level of spiritual obedience.

Recently, I absentmindedly misplaced my wallet. I wandered around the house upturning sofa cushions and digging through drawers. Cathy solved the puzzle by asking a simple question, "Where do you last remember having it?" Sure enough, as soon as I paused and recollected where I last had it, I found it again.

This is true spiritually. If you have lost the joy of Christ's presence, remember where you last had it. Trace your steps. Go back to that place and look again. Where did you veer off course? What was happening then that is not happening now? What are you doing or thinking now that you weren't doing or thinking then? Ask God to point out where you have detoured from his will. He will show you. God always helps honest seekers find their way back to the path.

## Free Refills

Living in the fullness of Christ's presence requires what Eugene Peterson calls "a long obedience in the same direction."[11] It's a lifetime commitment, not a one-time shot. We have to keep coming back for more.

Spirituality, like bread and milk, must be continually replenished. If not, we find ourselves with stale religion and sour sanctimony. We can't live on past commitments and victories. Yesterday's manna spoils and breeds maggots (Ex. 16:20).

Thankfully, God continually restores the soul (Ps. 23:3) and refreshes us with free refills.

## Trusting through Darkness

Sometimes, for unknown reasons, God seems distant and far removed from current reality. In fact, some of God's most treasured and dutiful saints are plagued with what St. John of the Cross called "the dark night of the soul."

For instance, letters from Mother Teresa to her superiors, published a decade after her death, revealed an inner struggle to feel God's blessing and presence. "There is so much contradiction in my soul," she lamented. "No faith—no love—no zeal . . . I find no words to express my pain."[12] Martin Luther often battled with what he called *anfechtungen*, a conflicted spiritual state, where God's absence seems greater than his presence, and his love appears somewhat questionable.[13] The desert monks referred to *acedia*, the dreaded "noonday demon," that describes a deep soul weariness and the serious malady of being unable to care.[14] Charles Spurgeon warned young preachers of "the minister's fainting fits," where all seems lost in the valley of despair.[15] From the cross, even Jesus cried, "My God, my God, why have you forsaken me?" (Matt. 27:46).

But even in his perceived absence, God is ever present.

A university philosophy professor wrote "God is nowhere" on the whiteboard. After class, one of the students grabbed a marker and drew a line between the w and the h, so the board said, "God is now / here."

When you feel like God is nowhere, rest assured, he is now here. The river is still there. "God is our refuge and strength, an ever-present help in trouble" (Ps. 46:1). Seek the Lord with all your heart, and you will find him.

But, if he doesn't seem to show up for some reason, then trust him with all your heart in the dark. "Let him who walks in the dark, who has no light, trust in the name of the LORD and rely on his God" (Isa. 50:10). If you keep on trusting through the darkness, he will bring you to the light.

## What Does It Look Like?

What does continuous immersion in Christ's presence look like? It's difficult to pinpoint because people are different with a wide variety of temperaments, backgrounds, gifts, and personalities. Christ's fullness in me looks different than his fullness in you.

Despite the differences, however, the essence is still the same. Christlikeness means flowing in the fullness of holy love, which is the constant river.

One powerful example I've observed is Dr. Wesley Duewel, president emeritus of OMS International. A few years ago, our congregation was transformed as we went through his devotional classic *Ablaze for God*. We invited Dr. Duewel, then age ninety-two, to

Hayward so he could share his heart and pray with us. To my delight, he accepted the invitation.

Obtaining special permission, I eagerly awaited Dr. Duewel's arrival at gate A19 of Minneapolis International Airport. His plane landed and a long line of passengers debarked—but no Wesley Duewel. The last stragglers came out of the tunnel, but there was still no sign of my special guest. I checked with the agent who radioed back into the plane and grunted, "He's coming. He's coming."

Finally, three flight attendants emerged from the jet bridge, and they were all wiping tears. One approached me. "Are you waiting for that precious little old man back there?" she blubbered. "He was just praying for us. It was so beautiful! I have never felt such love in all my life."

I was in awe. This holy man was so filled with God's loving presence that it automatically overflowed to everybody he met along the way. His very presence created a thin place for others, where heaven and earth merged together.

I lifted an eye toward heaven and prayed, "Lord, when I grow up, please make me the kind of guy who makes flight attendants cry."

But my righteous one will live by faith. And if he
shrinks back, I will not be pleased with him.

—Hebrews 10:38

# 5

# Faith

Filled with God's Promise

## A Fantastic Adventure

Late one night in a massive ice storm, I drove my sons Luke and
Wes from visiting a friend. White-knuckling the steering wheel, I
fretted as we crept homeward along the treacherous highway. Ice
pelted the windshield, making it difficult to see ahead.

As we passed our favorite sledding hill, the boys remembered
our sleds were in the trunk.

"Hey, Dad! Can you imagine how fast we could zip down that
hill tonight? Oh wow! That would be awesome! Let's do it! What
do you say Dad? Huh?"

"Uh—hmmm—I don't know, boys. That's a crazy idea. Can't
you see we're in the middle of a dangerous ice storm?"

"That's exactly the point Dad. We're here at the hill. Our sleds are with us, and that hill is slicker than ever. Don't you think we should take advantage of this opportunity?"

"Oh, why not?" I answered, tossing caution aside and hoping this decision wouldn't land somebody in the emergency room. "Just one time down, and then we need to get home."

We pulled out a three-person toboggan, struggled up the slippery precipice, and shoved off.

Luke and Wes yelled, "Yeah! Bonzai!"

I hung on for dear life and yelled too, "Yaaaaarrrrghhhh!"

Faster than an Olympian luge team, we hurtled down the hill and halfway across the frozen field at the bottom. My heart was in my stomach the whole way.

When we finally slowed to a stop, all three of us fell into the snow and laughed so hard our sides hurt.

"Dad, that's the coolest thing we've ever done."

I was just glad to survive.

"Let's do it again!"

We ended up going down the hill two more times. Walking back toward the car after our adventure in the pelting ice, I thought, "Sometimes, faith is like that. It requires a risk, is quite a ride, scares you half to death, and is guaranteed to make a memory." Corrie ten Boom said, "Faith is a *F*antastic *A*dventure *I*n *T*rusting *H*im.[1]

## Calmness in the Cabin

When you know you're following God's direction, stepping out in faith is not nearly so big a risk as one might imagine. It just *feels* like a risk. God's promise is as good as his character. When you have confidence that the Lord is on the throne, then having faith in him is no risk—only a fantastic adventure.

The passengers in the cabin of an airliner don't shriek in terror while they hurtle down the runway and catapult into the sky. Confidence in the captain brings calmness in the cabin.

When teaching my teens to drive, I have not always demonstrated such confidence and calmness. After an intense practice session behind the wheel, my son Wes turned off the ignition and said, "Dad, things would be a whole lot better if you quit grabbing the dash and yelling, 'Woah! Woah! Woah!'"

Obviously, there was neither confidence in the captain nor calmness in the cabin.

Fortunately, as my son's driving improved, so did my calmness. A few months after obtaining his license, Wes drove while I napped in the back seat. The confidence brought the calmness.

A leap of faith, then, is not so much a matter of risk, but a confidence in the captain, knowing that he will keep your feet firm. As John Greenleaf Whittier stated, "The foot of faith falls on the seeming void and finds the rock beneath."[2]

## Walking on Water

In Wisconsin's Northwoods, all Wesleyans walk on water. So do Baptists, Lutherans, and Catholics. Shoot, we don't just walk on water—we drive on it. Every February.

Each winter, little makeshift ice fishing villages pop up everywhere on area lakes. I've considered holding church out there on the ice, but the board hasn't gone along with me yet. I figure we can convert a few anglers, drill a big hole, and baptize them with bungee cords. We'll call it the Holy Jesus Polar Plunge.

The first winter after my arrival from sunny southern California, I couldn't believe my eyes when I saw people driving their pickups on the ice, heading for their fishing shanties. In December, I thought, "Those people are nuts!" In January, I just accepted it as natural part of tundra life. By February, I mustered up enough courage to join them.

While taking our family on a Sunday afternoon drive, I impulsively swerved our minivan onto the snow-packed trail toward Nelson Lake. There was no calmness in the cabin! All the kids yelled for dear life, and Cathy grabbed the dashboard, shouting "Woah! Woah! Woah!" But in a few moments, the panic subsided as we found ourselves gliding across the solid surface. Realizing the ice was definitely thick enough to hold us, they relaxed somewhat.

This incident reminded me of an old poem I've slightly revised from childhood:

A man walked out onto a frozen lake in trembling fear one day,
Then a four-wheel drive came rolling by, laughing all the way,
Great faith and little faith alike were granted safe convoy,
One had pangs of needless fear and the other had all the joy.[3]

Sometimes, forgetting how big God is, I end up fretting when I ought to be trusting, and can almost hear the voice of Jesus saying, "O, you of little faith."

## How Big Is God?

After the bedtime tucking one evening, my six-year-old son, Adam, asked, "Daddy, how big is God?"

"Really big," I replied.

"But *how* big, Daddy?"

"Super-duper big, Adam."

"Yes, Daddy, but how big is that?"

"Big enough," was my final answer. "God is big enough for anything."

The next day, I received distressing information regarding our church budget and sat behind my desk worrying it out with a pencil.

My anxious thoughts were interrupted by an unexpected rap at the door. Glenn Johnson, a godly elder of the congregation stood there smiling.

"Pastor," he said, "this morning in my prayer time, the Lord prompted me to drive to church and ask you this question: How big is God?"

I nearly fell off my seat. Relaying the prior evening's conversation, I said, "He's big enough, Glenn. He's big enough for anything."

## Lutefisk, Lent, and Great Faith

Northern Wisconsin is Lutheran and Catholic territory, and this means two things: Lutefisk before Christmas, and Lent before Easter. I didn't know much about either growing up. Until moving to Hayward, I had never heard of Lutefisk, and figured Lent was stuff you trap in the dryer.

Living in the Northwoods, I've discovered that Lutefisk is a piece of cod that passes all understanding. (Actually, it's a rather unappetizing, gelatinous Nordic dish made from dried, salted whitefish and lye.) We'll let the Lutherans keep it.

Lent, however, is something we've happily pilfered from our more liturgical brethren. We start with Ash Wednesday, forty days before Easter. I smudge ashes on the foreheads of willing parishioners, repeating, "From dust you've come, to dust you shall return."

For a few years, I drove over to St. Joe's a couple days before the Lenten season and borrowed ashes from my Catholic priest buddy, Father Bill. He pulled my leg when I asked him where he obtained the ashes. "From the funeral home, of course." He said it with such a straight face that I believed him at first.

When Father Bill retired, I lost my ash stash. Before leaving town, he finally divulged that the ashes come from last year's Palm Sunday branches. So now I hoard dead palm branches in my filing cabinet.

The first time I tried to burn palm branches, I nearly set the house on fire, and our smoke alarm shrieked. Cathy sent me and my pan of smoking palm fronds out the back door and instructed me to never burn them in the oven again. So, I've had to take my cremation operation outdoors.

It's fitting that the ashes are leftovers from Palm Sunday. We can't depend on yesterday's praises to get us through today's problems. Former glory fades to ashes and dust.

A couple of years ago, while smudging foreheads, I decided what to sacrifice for Lent. Normally, people give up stuff like candy, coffee, television, or Facebook in order test their spiritual resolve.

I gave up doubt. I determined that for forty days I would respond to every situation with this question: What would great faith have me do?

This commitment was tested immediately. In fact, I still had the ash smudge on my forehead when our high school pastor, Loretta, came bursting into my office with an exciting but expensive idea. Her enthusiasm bubbled over. "So, what do you think?" she asked eagerly. Dollar signs rolled in my head. How on earth were we going to pay for that? But I needed to keep my vow. What would great faith have me do? I gulped, grinned through gritted teeth, and replied, "Sure, what a splendid opportunity. Let's go for it."

And that's the way it went for the next forty days, responding to every situation with the greatest faith I could muster. Was I ever glad when Easter came, so I could go back to my old pattern of doubting and fretting!

Giving up doubt for Lent was one of the best decisions I've ever made, reminding me that true Christianity means living by faith every day. God is big enough to trust. The only way to be faithful is to be faith-full. "The just shall live by faith," the central theme of such spiritual giants as Augustine, Luther, and Wesley should be ours as well. "Without faith it is impossible to please God" (Heb. 11:6). Intuitively realizing we don't have enough, we share in the disciples' plea: "Increase our faith!" (Luke 17:5).

## How to Be Filled with Faith

How then, being called to "walk by faith, not by sight" (2 Cor. 5:7 NKJV), can we boldly believe and live the great adventure?

### Know What You Believe

The current decline of biblical Christianity in the Western world is alarming. A generic acceptance of vague spirituality is quickly replacing true knowledge of what we believe and why.

"Americans revere the Bible," researchers Gallup and Castelli concluded, "but, by and large, they don't read it. And because they don't read it, they have become a nation of biblical illiterates."[4]

Bible scholar, Dr. Albert Mohler, concurred: "While America's evangelical Christians are rightly concerned about the secular worldview's rejection of biblical Christianity, we ought to give some urgent attention to a problem much closer to home—biblical illiteracy in the church. This scandalous problem is our own, and it's up to us to fix it."[5]

The Bible provides the essential foundation for genuine faith. Christian faith does not exist apart from the Word. We won't live by it unless we know it. We won't know it unless we read and hear it. "So then faith *comes* by hearing, and hearing by the word of God" (Rom. 10:17 NKJV).

**Collecting Dust.** Most Christian families have several Bibles in the house collecting dust. While visiting the home of a family in his congregation, Pastor Tom requested that someone get their Bible so he could read a passage before departing. Mama turned to little Johnny and said, "Honey, would you go into my room and get that precious book I love so much and read every day?" Johnny returned carrying *TV Guide.*

That's typical. We've tuned in more to Hollywood than the Holy Word, leaving our souls shriveled and malnourished.

**The Real PowerPoint.** All pastors are under charge to "preach the Word" (2 Tim. 4:2) and "Christ crucified" (1 Cor. 1:23). There's nothing else to preach.

Don't preach your feeble opinions and philosophies. Don't just preach about the Bible. A real sermon is much more than that. It's literally proclaiming Scripture that speaks for itself, bringing powerful transformation to those who listen with open hearts. "The word of God is living and active" (Heb. 4:12).

My dad believed the Bible completely, lived by it authentically, and preached it passionately. He said, "Sermonettes, preached by preacherettes, produce Christianettes."

God's Word, declared boldly under Holy Spirit anointing, "shall not return . . . void" (Isa. 55:11 KJV).

I recall the great Wesleyan statesman Dr. Earle Wilson urging young pastors to stay true to Scripture in preaching: "Many pastors feel their sermons are lacking because their church can't afford the latest technology, video projection system, or PowerPoint." Then, waving his Bible high in the air, he thundered, "Pastor, *this* is your PowerPoint!"

## Believe What You Know

Professing Christians are called to live according to what the Scripture says. If your life doesn't match up, you have only two choices: reduce Scripture to fit your life, or adjust your life to fit Scripture. Regrettably, many professing Christians choose the first option. If my life doesn't match the Bible, I'll just bend the Bible.

A *Peanuts* cartoon depicted Charlie Brown shooting arrows at a fence. Lucy, who happened on the scene, was duly impressed that he had hit a perfect bull's-eye every time. She asked Charlie Brown to demonstrate his archery skills. Charlie grabbed an arrow, placed it on his bow, and fired it into the fence where there was no target. He then proceeded to the arrow and painted a target around it. "Charlie Brown, what are you doing?" Lucy asked. Charlie answered, "I'm making sure I never miss."

Many handle God's Word with the "shoot first, aim later" mentality. We may not actually say it, but our actions cry out, "We don't care what the Bible says. We're going to do our own thing anyway and ask God to bless it." In other words, instead of using the Scripture as our standard, we choose to stand apart, ignoring its authority.

**Amen to the Atheist.** Believers who don't believe aren't really believers. Even avowed skeptics understand this. The renowned atheist Christopher Hitchens was interviewed for the *Portland Monthly* by Unitarian minister Marilyn Sewell.

SEWELL: The religion you cite in your book is generally the fundamentalist faith of various kinds. I'm a liberal Christian, and I don't take the stories from the Scripture literally. I don't believe in the doctrine of atonement (that Jesus died for our sins, for example). Do you make any distinction between fundamentalist faith and liberal religion?

HITCHENS: I would say that if you don't believe that Jesus of Nazareth was the Christ and Messiah, and that he rose again from the dead and by his sacrifice our sins are forgiven, you're really not in any meaningful sense a Christian.

SEWELL: Let me go someplace else . . .[6]

I "amen" the atheist on that one! Of course, Scot McKnight reminds us, "We're all fundamentalists, but the issue is what our fundamental is. The Christian fundamental is a Man dying on a cross for his enemies. There's the truth."[7]

## Adjust Your Life to Match Up with the Bible

The only legitimate option, when facing a reality gap between the Bible and your life, is to adjust your life to match the Bible. You claim the Bible as God's Word, but do you really believe it? Are you putting all the faith you can into it? Are you practicing what it says?

A common place where our faith is tested is the area of finances. I don't understand why we get so worked up about little green pieces of paper with pictures of dead presidents on them. However, trusting God with our church budget has been my greatest faith challenge. Over the years the Lord has never failed us yet, but in weak moments I still find myself wondering if he will come through this time.

When facing fear, what you do next reveals what you really think about God.

## Plant the Faith Seed

Farmers understand the faith principle better than most people. They recognize it requires an upfront investment. Unless the seed falls to the ground and dies, it only remains a seed (John 12:24). You must take the risk and plant the seed in fertile soil to obtain a harvest. What you sow is what you grow. The righteousness tree won't flourish until you plant the faith seed.

Occasionally when our faith is weak, we can borrow someone else's. I have borrowed faith on many occasions and loaned mine out a few times as well.

I could not have walked into the hospital room at a better moment. The doctor had just left Gerry's room after informing him that he had terminal cancer. It was a devastating blow. Gerry was not a part of my church, but he was a friend, and I figured it would be good to pay him a visit. Little did I know how important that visit would become.

He unburdened his heart to me, and in the conversation I said, "Well in times like these, we need to draw on our faith."

"I'm sorry, but I don't have much faith," Gerry sighed.

I picked up a napkin from the tray next to his bed, and tore off a corner. Then, wadding it into a tiny little speck, I dropped it into Gerry's hand.

"That's the size of a mustard seed, Gerry. Do you have that much faith?" I asked.

"Well, yeah, of course, I've got *that* much faith,"

"Great!" I said, "The Bible says if you have faith the size of a mustard seed, you can move mountains. Let's take that little bit of faith you have, plant it in the soil of God's grace, and see what happens."

"OK, if you say so," said Gerry. He didn't sound convinced.

"And Gerry, if you don't have enough faith, I'll lend you some of mine."

The next week, when I went to visit Gerry in the hospital, I brought a real mustard seed with me. I swiped it from Cathy's spice cabinet. Walking toward the entrance, I accidently dropped the mustard seed in the parking lot. I crawled around for fifteen minutes on my hands and knees trying to find it, before finally giving up the quest.

Entering Gerry's room, I confessed, "I had some more faith for you Gerry, but I lost it in the parking lot." He grinned.

On Thanksgiving Day, our family had just sat down for our annual turkey feast, when the telephone rang. It was Gerry's nurse.

"Pastor, I hate to bother you on Thanksgiving, but Gerry asked me to call. He's dying and wants you to come. And he's mumbling something about mustard seeds."

That afternoon I drove to the hospital and prayed with Gerry, helping him find the assurance of salvation and peace in the face of death. He passed away a couple of hours later.

I am so thankful we planted that mustard seed together because now Gerry is experiencing life beyond life. A little bit of faith, packed with all God's promises, is always bigger than the problem, and it takes us on a great adventure in trusting him.

> But godliness with contentment is great gain.
>
> —1 Timothy 6:6

# 6

# Contentment

## Filled with God's Peace

### The Winter of Discontent

Northern Wisconsin winters are severe. Occasionally, in bleak midwinter, the mercury drops below minus forty Fahrenheit. Snow arrives in October, and blankets the ground in November, usually staying through Easter.

A couple of years ago, we had a blizzard on Easter weekend. The soloist at church sang, "Was It a Morning Like This?" and everybody chuckled as they pictured Jesus wading through knee-deep drifts on resurrection day. The morning before, two thousand bright plastic eggs were scattered across the snow-blanketed lawn for the big hunt. "Too easy to find," our children's pastor, Jeremy, declared. "Next year, we hide white eggs."

On the coldest days, we toss boiling water into the air and watch it crystallize before hitting the ground. We also blow soap bubbles, which instantly freeze and then roll around in the yard for hours without popping.

The winters are long, dark, and frigid.

For several months, the landscape is like a 1950s television set: black and white with lots of snow. Yet, most Northwoods folk are made of sturdy stock and take smug satisfaction in this endurance.

In northern Wisconsin, you won't survive if you don't embrace the winter.

Borrowing from Steinbeck via Shakespeare, I've noticed that some unhappy souls, in the dreaded struggle against the season, turn it into a long "winter of discontent."[1]

Many church leaders experience the work of ministry primarily as a winter of discontent. "If Satan's arsenal of weapons were restricted to a single one," said C. S. Lewis, "it would be discouragement."[2] Discouragement is evidence of a discontented root.

## Discontent: The Original Sin

This was the serpent's first lie in Eden. He stirred discontent within Adam and Eve, which led to doubt and then disobedience, partaking of forbidden fruit. They had everything they needed, but a desire for something else drew them away. As an old armchair philosopher once quipped, "Contentment isn't having what you want; it's wanting what you have."

As sons of Adam and daughters of Eve, we too are inclined to hear the whisperings and follow the same downward path of discontent, doubt, and disobedience. In the larger picture, all sin is rooted in discontent with God's kind care and loving provision.

Searching for satisfaction, significance, and security in anything beyond God is futile—leading only to deeper dissatisfaction, insignificance, and insecurity. This is why addictions are so prevalent today. We are attempting to meet deep spiritual needs with false substitutes.

Satan whispers, and we swallow the lie that our need for intimacy can be assuaged by online romances, extramarital affairs, or pornography. He whispers, and we falsely assume our pain will be relieved through intoxication. Satan whispers, and we wrongly believe our importance is based on performance and popularity. He whispers, and we mistakenly place our trust in financial stability and job security. He whispers, and we end up feeling unappreciated, unrecognized, and unrewarded.

Subtle whispers of discontent lure us from God alone as our source and sustainer.

## The Art of Divine Contentment

One March morning with a heavy spirit to match my load, I happened across a powerful little book from the seventeenth-century London puritan Thomas Watson, which transformed my perspective.

If anyone had a right to complain, it would have been Watson. After sixteen years of faithful service as rector of St. Steven's Walbrook, he was unfairly accused, deposed, and imprisoned because of his political views. Thomas Watson wrote a book in the midst of the persecution.

What kind of book would you write if you suffered unjustly under such conditions? I can imagine two or three books I'd be tempted to write: *It's Not Fair: A Plea for My Defense* or *Abuse of*

*Power: My Case against the King* or *Evil on the Throne: When Tyrants Rule.*

Watson, however, did not go that route. Instead, he penned a warm-hearted exposition on Philippians 4:11: "I have learned, in whatsoever state I am, therewith to be content" (KJV). The book was titled *The Art of Divine Contentment.*

The main point, according to the good rector, is that "a gracious spirit is a contented spirit. The doctrine of contentment is very superlative; and till we have learned this, we have not learned to be Christians."[3]

Watson then continued by listing three warning signs of discontent that (after figuring out what they meant) have helped me tremendously in measuring my own heart and assisting others in navigating life's perplexities. Using Watson's labels, I'll provide my own definitions.[4]

### Vexatious Repining

In simple language, this means fretting and stewing over problems, annoyances, and disruptions. It's working yourself into a dither.

Although potatoes and carrots improve greatly with stewing, troubles never do! Agitation and aggravation rarely help the situation.

Overreacting, bearing resentments, and blowing gaskets are as wrong as the original offence we're protesting. Perhaps this is what Jesus meant when he spoke of removing the plank from your own eye before attempting to remove the speck from your brother's (Matt. 7:5). Our sinful reaction is the plank.[5]

### Childish Despondency

This means being overburdened with cares—a heavy heartedness for the wrong reasons. It is like a canoe, overloaded with rocks, beginning to sink and take on water. Before attempting to navigate the river with such a heavy load, it might be better to ask why we're carrying all those rocks in the first place!

Once, in that misty state between wakefulness and sleep, I dreamed I was climbing a mountain with a heavy backpack on my shoulders, making the steep journey almost impossible. Then Jesus appeared on the path before me and asked why I was struggling so.

"My pack is too heavy," I complained. "I don't think I can make it."

Then Jesus gently said, "Let me see what I can do to help."

He proceeded to open the backpack and remarked, "No wonder it's so heavy! Why are you carrying these?"

Jesus removed two huge rocks from the pack and said, "You needn't haul these heavy things around." Then he hurled the rocks over the mountain's edge. My load was instantly lightened, and I joyfully resumed the upward journey.

Reflecting later, I labeled the rocks "fear" and "problems." I realized that in my ministry, I'd been carrying an unnecessary load. The weight of everybody's problems combined with fear of failure had overburdened my heart, leaving me frustrated and less effective in the pastoral work. Through that experience, God revealed that, although we are to carry one another's burdens (Gal. 6:2), we cannot absorb them. Instead, we are invited to carry them to Jesus (1 Pet. 5:7). "Cast your cares on the LORD and he will sustain you; he will never let the righteous fall" (Ps. 55:22).

Pastor Charles Tindley, counseling an anxious friend, said, "My advice to you is put all your troubles in a sack, take 'em to the Lord, and leave 'em there."[6]

## Uneven Discomposure

This is panic mode, imagining a worst-case scenario and then worrying it into existence.

Over the years, my kids accused me of this one, especially at meal times. A family of seven automatically means regular spills at the dinner table. For years, probably due to some deep-rooted psychological abnormality, every spill pushed my panic button. One of the kids would knock over a glass of milk, and instantly, I'd zoom into panic mode. Oh no! Spill! Get it! Get it! Rushing madly to the kitchen, I'd grab fistfuls of paper towels and dash urgently back to the table. My amused family would laugh as the drama unfolded. I think they enjoyed watching me run around like a chicken with my head cut off. In fact, I suspect a kid would knock something over on purpose occasionally just to get a rise out of me. In the aftermath of my table-spill eruptions, the kids gave me a nickname: Panicker Man! They even composed a little ditty to serenade me.

Recently though, with occasional slips, I've done much better at holding it in. Maybe it's because the kids are mostly grown now and spill less, or perhaps, it's just that I can't move as fast as I used to.

## The Secret of Contentment

How do we rid ourselves of such discontent? How do we find deep inner peace through life's struggles? The answer lies in finding our contentment in Jesus. John Piper rightly noted, "God is most glorified in us when we are most satisfied in Him."[7]

Contentment is not complacency or lazy reluctance. It is a call to active discipleship.

My favorite Bible verse, Philippians 4:13, reveals the secret of contentment: "I can do everything through him who gives me strength." I'll unpack this more in the next chapter, but for now, just understand the secret to contentment is dying to self.

We must willingly lay down our lives and go to the cross with Jesus. The "killing" precedes the filling. Our life prayer becomes, "Less of me and more of you." And when that happens, slowly but surely we begin to live in contentment with God's "good, pleasing and perfect will" (Rom. 12:2) as our selfish wants, desires, and opinions fade.

## I'm Gonna Die in Africa

A few years ago, I was invited to speak at a huge conference in Ethiopia, but a few days before departure, the event was abruptly cancelled. My missionary doctor friend Harold Adolph encouraged me, "You already have your ticket, so come to Africa anyway. We'll find something for you to do." So, I flew to Ethiopia, a land far different than Hayward, Wisconsin.

Dr. Adolph stopped the Jeep beside a remote lake during the journey to Soddo and pointed. "Look! There's a hippo snout sticking out of the water!" I leaned over and gazed intently, but couldn't quite see the snout. Just then, a mosquito buzzed near my face, and bit me on the cheek. "Uh oh!" I thought. "An Ethiopian mosquito bit me. Mosquitoes carry malaria. I'm going to get malaria. I'm going to die in Africa!"

In my imagination, that mosquito bite mushroomed to Everest proportions. I wondered what on earth a Northwoods boy like me was doing here in Ethiopia, staring at hippo snouts. And now, I was going to die in Africa.

Fortunately, the rest of the trip went better. I taught at a Bible college, encouraged the hospital staff, and conducted gospel seminars in a Muslim community. The highlight was preaching at their Sunday morning worship service. One of the church leaders picked me up at 7:30 a.m., and when we arrived at the church, I was astounded by the crowd already assembled. A thousand people packed the simple frame structure, singing praises. Another two thousand, unable to fit inside, surrounded the building, joining in the jubilant praise. Back home, the coffee pot is barely brewing at 7:30 on Sunday morning, but in Ethiopia, the worship is already in full swing.

Moments before I preached, one of the elders whispered to me that their leader had been brutally martyred by the communists several years before. "We bought the land where our pastor was buried," he explained, "and the pulpit now stands directly over his grave." I marveled, recalling Tertullian's observation that the blood of the martyrs is the seed of the church.

They ushered me to the pulpit, where I enthusiastically delivered my sermon through an interpreter. Every line of the message was met with thunderous cheers and exuberant shouts of "Alleluia!" and "Amen!" That doesn't usually happen in Hayward.

Then, after the sermon, the choir led the vast congregation in a rousing number with an African beat and shouts of joy. The interpreter leaned over and whispered, "They're singing your sermon right now. They're making up the song on the spot. It helps them remember what they learned today." I guess the traditional hymn or praise song controversy passed by them unnoticed. Every Sunday is a new song.

Sitting on the platform, as my Ethiopian brothers and sisters sang my sermon, the Holy Spirit convicted my heart. "Remember a few days ago when the mosquito bit you and you thought you were going to die in Africa? That's exactly what I've called you here to do. Right here. Right now, in Africa. You need to die to yourself!" Sometimes, the preacher needs the sermon more than the congregation.

As the music continued, I fell to my knees and surrendered my heart anew to God, as he revealed my unholy ambitions, attitudes, and perspectives that needed to go. I died to me.

Rising renewed, tears flowed down my cheeks and I shared the apostle Paul's testimony: "I have been crucified with Christ and I no longer live, but Christ lives in me" (Gal. 2:20). It was one of the most moving and cathartic experiences of my life. I will never forget the day I died in Africa.

## Dead Men Don't Panic

Several hours later, the missionaries dropped me off at the Addis Ababa airport, with cheerful farewells and reassurances that I'd be just fine. I approached the ticket counter to check in, but the agent clucked his tongue, shook his head ruefully and said, "I am very sorry, sir, but you did not call and confirm you ticket yesterday, so we gave your seat to another."

"Well, OK," I replied. "Then how about if you give me another seat?"

"Oh, I am so sorry, sir. This plane is completely full. We can probably book you on our next flight."

"Great!" I said. "And what time does the next flight go out?"

"The day after tomorrow," the agent replied.

I gulped, "The day after tomorrow?"

Mr. Panicker Man kicked in. What was I going to do? How would I survive two whole days in this strange place, with no way to contact my missionary friend, and very little cash in my pocket? Then the Holy Spirit spoke to my heart again. "Remember this morning? You died in Africa!"

"Yes, Lord," I replied.

"Dead men don't panic!"

The power of that simple concept hit me like a lightning bolt. Of course I won't panic! I'm a dead man! I cannot describe the sense of peace and release that flooded over me instantly. In that unusual, uncomfortable, uncertain situation, my heart was filled and overflowing with contentment. My perspective changed immediately. I thought, "Since I'm already a dead man, nothing can harm me. I might as well enjoy the journey." In renewed confidence that everything would work out somehow, I went with the flow.

The experience reminded me of Stormie Omartian's prayer, "Lord, help me to be content with where I am, knowing that You will not leave me there forever."[8]

At the final boarding call, I tried one last shot with the ticket agent. "You are a very lucky man," he beamed. "One seat just opened up."

I took it and returned home filled with contentment and peace— in the first row of first class right next to the Ethiopian ambassador to the United Nations.

## RIP

A frazzled mother continually complained about her stress level. "I just need some peace and quiet!" she groaned. So, for Mother's Day, her daughter Jessica went to the florist shop and returned proudly carrying the perfect gift for her mother. The arrangement included a pink bow inscribed, "Rest in Peace."

Leonard Sweet and Frank Viola, in their groundbreaking book *Jesus Manifesto*, said, "Knowing Christ as your 'rest' and allowing Him to live His life through you is one of the most freeing things you can know as a Christian."[9] They continue, "Resting in Christ doesn't mean being passive. It means allowing the Lord to do the heavy lifting.[10]

"Let the beloved of the LORD rest secure in him, for he shields him all day long, and the one the LORD loves rests between his shoulders" (Deut. 33:12).

## Divine Discontent

Of course, in all this contentment talk, we must remember that there is a place for discontent as well. Holy obedience often leads to divine discontent.

We should never be content with:

- a sin pattern in our lives,
- allowing the defenseless to suffer injustice,
- spiritual stagnation and yesterday's grace,
- doing church without community transformation,
- a hurting world that does not know God's love,
- anemic prayers,
- fruitless ministry,
- just repeating what we did last year,
- failing to reach out to lost and broken people, and
- settling for the status quo.

Authentic Christ followers are naturally discontent with anything that falls short of God's glory. Bill Hybels correctly noted, "You can't read the New Testament without seeing some of these 'discontentedness-producing' issues crop up."[11]

Regardless of how much discontent we feel at the edges, it's imperative to keep centered in contentment. Focusing more on what's wrong with the world rather than what's right with Jesus sinks the spirit. Only by keeping contentment at the center can we leverage holy discontent for positive change.

A rescue raft can't assist drowning victims if it springs a leak. In the end, it doesn't matter how deep the water is, as long as the water stays out of the boat. When we're airtight, we won't be uptight. An airtight heart, filled with contentment and peace, is the best possible craft for sailing into deep waters to rescue the perishing.

## Praise Gets You Airborne

Praising the Lord is the quickest way to find contented peace. On many occasions when I'm heavyhearted, I look to heaven and say, "Well, praise the Lord!" Somehow, the situation seems better by praising.

Taxiing on the runway before a flight to Pittsburgh, I read the following passage from *Knocked Down, But Not Out* by the dynamic Pentecostal preacher Billy Joe Daugherty: "Why should we praise God? Because we already know the outcome! Praise will cause the enemy to go into confusion. Praise is what gets you airborne. A lot of people are just taxiing up and down the runway saying, 'I'm a' hopin' and a' prayin'. You all pray with me.' Get off the runway and turn on the praise: 'Lord, I praise You. I thank You that You have redeemed me! You are going to make a way for me where there seems to be no way!' Suddenly, you are airborne and you are on your way!"[12]

I turned to the salesman sitting next to me, "Look at this! Look at this! It talks about taxiing on a runway—and that's exactly what we're doing. It says praise gets you airborne. Let's do it. Let's say, 'Praise the Lord!' when we take off." My seatmate was a good sport, and we both raised our hands and hollered, "Praise the Lord!" as the plane lifted into the sky.

## Contentment and Peace

There is a direct link between peace and contentment. Colossians 3:15, for example, begins with "Let the peace of Christ rule in your hearts" and ends with "be thankful." Peace with God is the secret to contentment.

My friend Barb shared this common couplet at a funeral recently: "No Jesus, no peace. Know Jesus, know peace." Yes, peace with God is the secret to contentment, and contentment is the secret to the peace *of* God.

When our hearts are at peace with God, we discover deep contentment: a peace that passes all understanding.

## The Fence of Trust

One afternoon, I found myself sitting alone in the cavernous old sanctuary of First Presbyterian Church in Duluth, Minnesota. Several burdens weighed me down, and numerous issues clouded my mind. I desperately needed to refocus and find God's peace.

A beautiful stained glass window caught my attention. It memorialized a young mother, Sarah Agnes Graf, who passed away suddenly in 1889, leaving her beloved husband, Philip, and five children. I've heard it said that there are two things that pierce the heart: beauty and anguish. This haunting window captured both. The following words, inscribed at the bottom, strengthened my weary soul:

Build a little fence of trust around today;
Fill the space with love and work and therein stay.
Look not through the sheltering bars upon tomorrow;
God will help thee bear whatever comes of joy or sorrow.[13]

The truth is that life and ministry are filled with good times and bad, mountaintops and valleys, smooth sailing and rough waters. You can't always have the one or completely avoid the other. So the key to doing all God would have us do and being all he has called us to be is total trust, total peace, and total contentment.

# 7

# Enduement

## Filled with God's Power

## Do Everything through Christ

My favorite Bible verse, as noted in the previous chapter, is Philippians 4:13: "I can do everything through him who gives me strength." At first I considered this verse a Lombardian locker-room speech. "You can do it if you set your minds to it. Go, fight, win! I can do *everything* through Christ!" The problem is that trying to do everything leads to failure. You'll flop miserably attempting great things for God in the power of the flesh. Trying to do everything accomplishes nothing.

Friends of the afflicted often say, "God will never give you more than you can handle." That's not true. God gives us all sorts of things we can't handle, but he'll never give us more than *he* can handle.

Focus on the last part of Philippians 4:13 rather than the first: "through him [Christ] who gives me strength." Feeble human effort accomplishes little. We need an enduement of supernatural power.

## Enduement Recognition

My computer doesn't recognize the word *enduement*. Most people don't recognize it either as it has been mothballed in the ecclesiastical attic for nearly a century. There is something we do recognize, however: our woeful lack of power to accomplish great spiritual work. Wesley Duewel said,

Over many a Christian leader's record could be stamped these words: LACKS POWER. Why do so many ministers and lay leaders have a vague restless awareness that something is lacking in their leadership? They have had adequate training; they make all the needed preparation; they work faithfully and hard. But it all remains largely on the human level.

If you rely on training, you accomplish what training can do. If you rely on skills and hard work, you obtain the results that skills and hard, faithful work can do. When you rely on committees, you get what committees can do. But when you rely on God, you get what God can do."[1]

We desperately need to realize this word we don't recognize. *Enduement* means an extraordinary filling of spiritual power for life, witness, and service.

## Enduement for Mr. Toad

One sweaty August afternoon, my lawn mowing was interrupted by seven-year-old Hannah who bounded toward me, waving her arms wildly. "Help, Daddy! Help!"

Stopping the mower, I turned to her and asked, "What do you need?"

"Can you help me get the toad off the roof of the shed?"

"Huh? How on earth did a toad get on top of the shed?"

"He jumped."

"Now, Hannah," I reasoned, "you and I both know toads can't jump that high. Now tell me, how did that toad get on the roof?"

Beaming, she replied, "I helped him jump."

What a surprise for Mr. Toad. He was just sitting around minding his own business, when a power beyond himself took over and he achieved heights previously unknown.

Landing on that shed roof, the startled amphibian must have thought, "I didn't know I had it in me." One could say, at that moment, Mr. Toad received an enduement of power.

## Slower than Gilbert Brown

A few years ago our family visited the Green Bay Packers training camp, to watch our gridiron heroes and collect a few autographs. Right across the street from the practice field, the team sponsored a special tourist attraction called The Packer Experience. For a not-so-nominal fee, fans were invited to become imaginary Packers. After some arm twisting, I relented and took the gang in to join the team. We tried on shoulder pads, wore authentic jerseys, tossed a game-used football, had our knees taped, and received black smudges under our eyes. The Packer Experience included a forty-yard dash, where sprinting fans were clocked and compared with Packers players.

"Dad, let's see you do it," my kids urged.

"Nah," I replied, "I don't want to show anybody up."

"Oh, c'mon Dad. Be a good sport. Go for it!"

So, I did.

I hunched over the starting line and at the signal took off like a shot, running as fast as my squatty little legs could go. Music from *Chariots of Fire* echoed in my mind.

My grinning kids stood at the finish. To congratulate me? Not a chance! They were just waiting to have some fun at my expense. As I crossed the line, they doubled over, howling with laughter.

"Dad!" they hooted, "you're slower than Gilbert Brown!"

Now, Gilbert Brown was a monster lineman, pushing four hundred pounds. His bigness was legendary—so big, a Green Bay restaurant advertised giant-sized Gilbert Burgers on the menu. Ol' Gilbert was by far the slowest player on the team—and I was slower than him. Might as well paste a "Slow Moving Vehicle" sign on my back.

A few weeks later, however, I was in a Boeing 737 flying to a speaking engagement. The little information guide in the seat pocket said we travelled at 585 miles per hour. I thought, "Who's going faster now, Gilbert Brown?" Gilbert couldn't touch that. I was going faster than the fastest Packer! My travel at such super-human speed was entirely due to a power far beyond my own. My job was to board the plane, and the pilot took care of the rest.

And *that's* what the enduement of spiritual power does, enabling us to accomplish far more than we could on our own. "'Not by might nor by power, but by my Spirit,' says the LORD Almighty" (Zech. 4:6).

## The Prayer of Enduement

At the annual ordination service, seasoned ministers in black suits huddle around the ordinands, laying their hands on them and speaking the prayer of enduement: "Our Father, we beseech You to send upon these Your servants Your heavenly blessings: that they may be clothed with righteousness and with the power of the Holy Spirit, that Your Word spoken in their mouths may have success and that it may never be spoken in vain. . . . Assist us, O Lord, in all our doings, with Your most gracious favor, and further us with Your continual help, that in all our works begun, continued and ended in You, we may glorify Your holy name . . . through Jesus Christ our Lord. Amen."[2]

When they laid hands on me and prayed this, I had goose bumps, but other than that, the results weren't too spectacular. My ministry over the next few years was primarily a work of the flesh, until I totally surrendered everything and received a fresh fullness of the Spirit in my life. Only then did I understand what the prayer of enduement was supposed to mean.

## My Re-Ordination

Dr. Bob McIntyre, a godly man who once led the National Association of Evangelicals, presided over many ordinations as general superintendent of The Wesleyan Church. Sometime after his retirement, Dr. McIntyre showed up unexpectedly at my church one Sunday morning.

When the service ended, I invited him to my study, shared my recent spiritual experiences, and asked if he would pray the prayer of enduement over me again. "It didn't take the first time," I explained, "and now that I know what it means, I need it more than ever." Dr. McIntyre graciously agreed, and we held my own little re-ordination right there in my office. We need this special empowering for ministry. It's one thing to pray it in an ordination service; it's quite another to experience it personally.

The enduement is not just for ordained pastors. Every believer needs it. The call to follow Jesus always leads to ministry of some sort, and we all need power for that. "Either you are a minister or you need one."[3] (Of course, when you're a minister, you still need one.)

## Fully Clothed

*Endue* sounds almost like the Greek word it came from. It basically means "to clothe."

Dr. Leslie Wilcox conducted an in-depth study on the word and discovered that of the couple dozen times it is used in the New Testament, thirteen refer to literal wearing of garments, five refer to the resurrection body, and the others refer to figurative clothing of a spiritual nature:

- Clothed with spiritual armor (Eph. 6:11, 13; Rom. 13:12; 1 Thess. 5:8)
- Clothed with the new self (Eph. 4:24)
- Clothed with the Lord Jesus Christ (Rom. 13:14)
- Clothed with compassion, kindness, humility, gentleness, patience, and love (Col. 3:12, 14)
- Clothed with power from on high (Luke 24:49)[4]

Wilcox then summarized, "Does not this list give a splendid example of what the enduement means? . . . This certainly indicates a new quality of life, a new protection from the attacks of evil, a new power to withstand such attacks, and a new and deeper manifestation of the Christ-spirit, when the believer is endued with power from on high."[5]

## What Holds Us Back?

If such power is available to us, then why aren't we tapping into it? What blocks the spiritual flow in our lives? One simple thing: We're holding back. We're not willing to do whatever it takes to get out of the way and let the Spirit flow.

Oswald Smith was onto something when he said, "I often think of the Holy Spirit as a mighty river, but a river dammed and held back by obstacles of one kind and another. Fancy a man standing on the dam and pleading in prayer with the river to flow on. How absurd! 'Why,' the river would answer, 'that is just what I want to do. Don't waste your energy in such vain repetitions. It is my nature to flow. I'm more anxious to flow than you are to see me flow.'"[6]

Christ's power ceases flowing at the point of our reluctance and self-will. It is available to all, but too often, like the rich young ruler, we turn away sorrowfully. We love ourselves more than we love Christ. God stands ready to empower every sincere seeker who turns to him without reservation. Through his fullness, we receive a special enduement for victory, fruitfulness, wisdom, and service.

# Power to Overcome

The Holy Spirit brings victory over sin, self, and circumstances. Maybe we should call it "En-DON'T-ment": empowered to say "no" to the lure of temptation.

## Overcoming Sin

"What is the quickest way to get rid of temptation?" the Sunday school teacher asked.

One kid blurted, "Give in to it."

I suppose that's one way. Many spiritual strugglers assume giving in is the only option. However, the apostle John said quite the contrary: "I write this to you so that you will not sin" (1 John 2:1). The enduement of power gives victory over temptation.

Following John Wesley's conversion, he remarked, "After my return home, I was much buffeted with temptations; but cried out, and they fled away. They returned again and again. I as often lifted up my eyes, and He 'sent me help from his holy place.' And herein I found the difference between this and my former state chiefly consisted. I was striving, yea, fighting with all my might under the law, as well as under grace. But then I was sometimes, if not often, conquered; now, I was always conqueror."[7]

## Overcoming Self

Humility is the practice of overcoming self. You can't be full of yourself and full of Jesus too.

D. L. Moody said, "God sends no one away empty except those who are full of themselves."[8] The Spirit doesn't abide with selfish pride, which is the source of most conniptions.

A good test of spiritual maturity is examining what upsets you.

### Overcoming Circumstances

Do you love all the great promises of Scripture? How about this one? John 16:33 says, "In this world you will have trouble." Now, isn't that disheartening? Yet it's reality. There's no such thing as trouble-free living, and that's a promise.

Troubles come in the form of problems or facts of life. There is a difference between the two. A problem is something you can solve. A fact of life is something you must accept. We're bound to have plenty of both.

Thankfully, this promise is sandwiched between two others in the same verse that far outweigh it: "In me you may have peace" and "Take heart! I have overcome the world."

## Power to Produce

The fruit of the Spirit does not come by trying hard to produce fruit, but only by yielding and infilling. We open our lives in surrender to Christ, and he produces the fruit. Have you ever seen a tree straining to grow apples? Of course not! Apple trees just sink their roots deep for nourishment, and the fruit comes as a byproduct. As Dallas Willard says, "The apple tree naturally and easily produces apples because of its inner nature."[9] The root generates the fruit.

Officiating a recent wedding, I asked the couple, "Wouldn't you agree that a marriage should be filled with love, joy, and peace? Shouldn't your relationship be characterized by patience, kindness, and goodness? Do you hope to have a marriage marked by faithfulness, gentleness, and self-control? Everybody nodded. Of course that's what a good marriage should be.

I told the bride and groom that this is fruit produced only by the Holy Spirit (Gal. 5:22–23). "If you want these things to describe your relationship, then you must humbly ask Christ to fill your marriage with his Spirit. You won't get it any other way."

You won't get more love by trying to be more loving. You won't become more patient by trying to be more patient. You won't be more self-controlled by trying harder to control yourself. These come from the Spirit-filled life. Deep roots, sweet fruits.

## Power to Discern

By power to discern, I don't mean being negative and judgmental. *Discernment* is sometimes used to spiritualize cantankerousness. John Wesley said such critics "instead of joining together against the common enemy, have turned their weapons against each other, and so not only wasted their precious time, but hurt one another's spirits, weakened each other's hands, and so hindered the great work of their common Master!"[10]

Rather, discernment is the demonstration of wisdom. The Hebrew word most frequently translated *discernment* is also used for *understanding*. The fullness of Christ filters thoughts, words, and deeds with wise understanding.

An old bard once said, "He that thinketh by the inch, and speaketh by the mile, ought to be kickethed by the foot." Proverbs 23:7 says, "As he thinketh in his heart, so is he" (KJV). Jesus died to take away our sins, not our brains.

Holy discernment helps us beyond right and wrong, beyond wise and foolish. It also fine-tunes the subtle differences between good and best. "And this is my prayer: that your love may abound more and more in knowledge and depth of insight, so that you may be able to discern what is best and may be pure and blameless until the day of Christ" (Phil. 1:9–10).

We need the enduement of the Holy Spirit for making godly decisions, speaking edifying words, and taking captive every thought in obedience to Christ (2 Cor. 10:5). "But when he, the Spirit of truth, comes, he will guide you into all truth" (John 16:13).

## Power to Serve

The enduement of power produces extraordinary results in service and ministry. God accomplishes great things through those who simply make themselves available. He often chooses those who seem the least likely to do his will:

- Moses, the fugitive sheep farmer on the backside of nowhere
- Esther, the Jewish teenager, suffering from injustice and prejudice
- Zacchaeus, the vertically challenged tax collector

When God chooses a "least likely" to do his best work, everybody knows it is divine power rather than human ability that does it.

One person empowered by the Holy Spirit can accomplish more than a hundred serving by human ability alone. Consider the great faith heroes of Scripture and history who yielded to God and achieved great exploits as the Spirit flowed through them.

The work of ministry, as mentioned earlier, can be summed up in four words: *love*, *lead*, *pray*, and *preach*. We need a special empowerment for these duties. Without them, our service will only be according to the flesh, and that will fail us.

### Empowered Loving

The fullness of the Spirit brings power to love everybody—even our enemies. This enduement brings the supernatural ability to forgive as Christ forgives and to rise above resentment.

I often tell ministerial students, "A minister must relinquish the right to bear offense." Some react negatively to this statement. They think it is too difficult, but that is because they are assuming they have to release resentments on their own. In the human dimension, this attitude is unattainable, but Christ's power makes it possible.

Christ is the lover flowing through you. Christ loves and you are the vessel.

### Empowered Leading

God's "gracings" accompany his "placings." He often puts people in positions where responsibility exceeds ability to prove his power and teach lessons in trust, wisdom, and humility. Spiritual authority for such service comes only comes through the Spirit's indwelling in the path of holy love.

Christ is the leader flowing through you. Christ leads and you are the vessel.

### Empowered Praying

"The effective, fervent prayer of a righteous man avails much" (James 5:16 NKJV). When our hearts are right with God and we're tapped into the source, we have praying power.

Weakness and shallowness in the prayer closet results in weak and shallow prayers with others. Thankfully, the Holy Spirit is available to infuse and help our praying (Rom. 8:26–27).

Christ is the prayer flowing through you. Christ prays and you are the vessel.

### Empowered Preaching

Teaching and preaching ring hollow unless anointed by the Spirit. The old timers called this anointing "unction."

Without it, our most creative and eloquent efforts will produce little harvest. Unction-less preaching is wading through the weeds. With unction, something supernatural occurs.

The Holy Spirit is the preacher flowing through you. Christ preaches and you are the vessel.

## Crazy Straws

I once brought a package of crazy straws home. My kids thought they were really cool until they went through the dishwasher and the insides glommed up. The next time they tried using them, nothing came through.

Sipping refreshment, we never brag, "What a fantastic straw." Instead we say, "Mmmm, what a delicious drink." The only time we pay attention to a straw is if the juice isn't getting through.

The same thing applies to preachers and other church workers. At the end of the day, the hearers should be saying, "What a great Savior," rather than, "What a great preacher." Preachers and teachers who make themselves the point are just glommed up crazy straws.

Our job is to get out of the way and let God flow through us.

## Artesian Well

Two humble Free Methodist ladies, Auntie Cook and Mrs. Snow, approached young D. L. Moody after he had preached, and said, "We are praying for you."

"Why are you praying for me? Why don't you pray for the unsaved?" the irritated evangelist replied.

"We are praying that you might get the power."

God used this interaction to spur Moody toward a deeper spiritual life. He hungered for the fullness of the Spirit and, after an earnest quest, received a mighty anointing. "The power of God fell upon him as he walked up the street and he had to hurry off to the house of a friend and ask that he might have a room by himself, and in that room he stayed alone for hours; and the Holy Ghost came upon him filling his soul with such joy that at last he had to ask God to withhold His hand, lest he die on the spot from very joy."[11]

From that moment forward, Moody's ministry was transformed. His biographer observed, "The fruits of his preaching had been small and few. . . . He had been trying to *pump* water out of a well that seemed dry. . . . He pumped with all his might, but little water came. . . . Then God made his soul like an *Artesian* well that could never fail of water."[12]

## Untapped Resource

A tourist marveling at the wild and unrestrained power of Niagara Falls exclaimed, "That must be the greatest untapped power resource in North America."

To this his companion replied, "No, the greatest untapped resource is the power of the Holy Spirit."

When you tap into this power source, you will find renewed energy and vigor for serving Jesus. "To this end I labor, struggling with all his energy, which so powerfully works in me (Col. 1:29).

> Pray without ceasing.
> —1 Thessalonians 5:17 (KJV)

# 8

# Confluence

## Prayer Is the Filling Station

As a small-town pastor, I've been called on to say prayers at graduation ceremonies, ski races, birthday parties, pet blessings, military deployments, auctions, a sculpture unveiling, and even a hockey tournament.

I'm learning there's much more to the prayer adventure than saying prayers. God is helping me become a man of prayer. There's a big difference between speaking words and living the prayer life.

During an extremely stressful situation, I knelt in my room, informing God of everything that was wrong. After fifteen minutes of blathering, realization struck: I wasn't praying—just fretting with my eyes closed. Effective prayer isn't telling God how big my problem is, but telling my problem how big God is.

Reading biographies of such faith heroes as David Brainerd, George Mueller, Corrie ten Boom, Amy Carmichael, R. A. Torrey, and others, I am always inspired by how they prayed. Their prayer-saturated lives reveal this important truth: You cannot live well unless you pray well. Godliness is the fruit of deep, frequent, and fervent praying. Prayerful means prayer-full.

Prayer is not parsley garnish on the platter. It is the main dish—the steak and potatoes. Rather than a token gesture, prayer is our chief source of spiritual strength.

Untangling a perplexing problem at a church board meeting, a member suggested, "Maybe we should stop and pray about this."

Another gasped, "Oh, no! Has it really come to that?"

Too often, we consider prayer a last resort, living by the adage, "When all else fails, try praying." Maybe we'd fail less if we prayed first!

## Outgrowing Your Prayer Life

My friend Tom Albin, dean of the Upper Room Ministries, recently challenged a group of Christians by asking, "If I told you that we are going to spend the next thirty minutes in prayer, how would you respond? Honestly, deep in your soul, what is your gut-level response? I know some of you would say, 'Oh, good! I can hardly wait. To pray for thirty minutes in the presence of other Christians will be wonderful.' Others would say, 'Thirty whole minutes? Oh my goodness, what am I supposed to do with the other twenty-eight? After two minutes, I have nothing left to pray.'"

Tom then made this observation: "If the idea of praying for a half hour does not delight you, then there's a good chance you have outgrown your prayer practices. It is time for you to learn new and better ways to pray."[1]

When we love someone deeply, we eagerly anticipate spending time together. The communication is pure delight. Consider a young couple in love: They spend countless hours in deep communication and don't seem bothered or bored. Should we not take such pleasure in spending time with our Savior, the one who loves us most?

## The Most Important Job

"The three most important things you can do," said Billy Graham, "are to pray, pray, pray!"[2] Prayer is the most significant work of ministry and our greatest act of love. Anybody is welcome to participate.

My friend George Voss resides at Water's Edge Nursing Home. His body has been ravaged by diabetes and strokes, leaving him blind in one eye, crippled in both hands, and unable to walk. Yet George is actively involved in the most important work of the church. He is a prayer warrior, and his intercession is as valuable as anything anybody else does.

In fact, I'd rather have one prayer warrior like George who can't usher, play guitar, or sit on a committee, than a thousand ushers, guitar strummers, or committee sitters who don't pray. E. M. Bounds said, "The prayers of God's saints are the capital stock in heaven by which Christ carries on His great work upon earth."[3]

## Become a Prayer Champion

What you are in prayer before God is what you are—nothing more. Your spiritual character rises and falls on the depth of your prayer life. Most believers settle for anemic praying because they've failed to develop the daily practice.

Like other Green Bay Packers fans in Wisconsin, I've observed that a championship team must possess three essential character-istics: a good running game, the ability to throw deep, and a solid defense. Similar qualities are important for anyone desiring to become a prayer champion.

## Praying on the Run

It is possible to carry a spirit of prayer throughout your daily routine. You can bring Jesus with you to work, the gym, the store, and the coffee shop. He is ready to meet you in life's common, ordinary happenings.

This is especially important for those whose schedules prohibit long periods of quiet solitude—such as mothers with infants and toddlers.

**Prayer Diapers.** Back when we had kids in diapers, Cathy lamented to our small group that she struggled to carve out time to pray. "No matter how early I rise, the baby gets up earlier. It's non-stop until I collapse in bed, exhausted, with hardly a moment between bottles and battles. Finding time to pray is hard when your whole life is consumed with changing diapers."

"Every diaper is a prayer, young lady," John, a feisty grandpa, asserted. "Anything done for the love of God is prayer, and don't you ever forget that!"

The spiritual implications of dirty diapers tickled my funny bone, but struck a deep chord with Cathy, affirming her labors and reminding her of God's special grace for those facing the messes of motherhood. At about 2:00 a.m. the next morning, when the baby squalled, Cathy nudged me and said, "Prayer time."

**Practicing the Presence.** John's dirty diaper prayer challenge reminded me of Brother Lawrence, the seventeenth-century Carmelite monk, who peeled potatoes and washed dishes in the monastery kitchen for over half a century. Because of his demanding job, he was not often released to attend public prayer services. So, he decided to turn the kitchen into his sanctuary and developed a way of life that he called "practicing the presence of God." Before long, news of Brother Lawrence spread, and pilgrims streamed to the busy kitchen for a blessing.

"The time of business does not with me differ from the time of prayer," said the happy monk. "And in the noise and clatter of my kitchen, while several persons are at the same time calling for different things, I possess God in as great tranquility as if I were upon my knees at the blessed sacrament."[4] Our heavenly Father cares about life's details, thus it is totally appropriate to invite him into all of them. Andrew Murray said, "If the Lord Himself will keep the soul night and day, yes, will watch and water it every moment, then surely the uninterrupted communion with Jesus becomes a blessed possibility to those who can trust God to mean and to do what He says."[5]

## Pray Deep

Without diminishing the importance of living in a constant spirit of prayer, I must say that the pressing need of today's church is for her leaders to pray deeply. Pastors frequently find themselves so caught up in changing "spiritual diapers" that, like overwhelmed mothers, they don't find time to draw aside for reflection and replenishing.

Now, some bivocational pastors who endure long, grueling days of full-time employment in addition to church work are granted a special dispensation. Due to a schedule beyond their control, the only option is to pray on the run. Most ministers, however, have no excuse for failing to go deep in prayer. Our only hindrances to taking significant time in communion with God are unwillingness and weakness of the flesh. We pray as much as we want, and obviously, we don't want it enough.

E. M. Bounds, in his spiritual classic *Preacher and Prayer,* said, "Every preacher who does not make prayer a mighty factor in his [or her] own life and ministry is weak as a factor in God's work and is powerless to project God's cause in the world."[6] One cannot be a true spiritual leader without spiritual power, and this is only attained through much prayer.

**Prayer Giants.** Heroes of the holy life have all been mighty in prayer. Consider the following examples:

- John Wesley spent two hours a day in prayer.
- Richard Baxter is said to have stained the walls of his room by the breath of his prayers.
- John Hyde would get so lost in intercession that he would forgo food, sleep, and other physical comforts.
- Martin Luther said that he had so much business he could not get on without spending three hours daily in prayer.
- Edward Payson reportedly wore grooves in his hardwood floors through ceaseless praying.
- David Brainerd prayed in knee-deep snow so long and vigorously that the snow around him melted.

To be honest, I read such reports with ambivalence. Two contradicting feelings rage within me: (1) Ugh, how discouraging! There's no way I could ever pray like that; and (2) Wow, how inspiring! I want to deepen my prayer life! When thinking straight about these mighty prayer warriors, I feel like a high school quarterback visiting the NFL Hall of Fame. Instead of being intimidated and defeated, I marvel at their exploits and dream of possibilities.

**Prayer Commitments.** Through the examples of these great prayer champions, the crucible of painful experience, and my frustrations with feeble ministry efforts, I've learned the importance of prayerfulness for joyful, fruitful ministry. This required some significant schedule adjustments, as calendars reflect priorities.

I made the following commitments in order to build prayer into the fabric of my daily life:

- Seek the face of God before seeking the face of people.
- No Facebook until I've faced the Book.
- No food for my stomach until my soul has been fed.
- Knee-mail before e-mail.
- Waking early means getting up to be with him. No rolling over and going back to sleep.
- The Bible, my journal, a hymnal, poetry, and other spiritual reading are allowed. Other literature (such as self-help or leadership books) is not permitted during my early watch.

I don't pretend to be a Hall of Fame hero like the saints listed above, but I am striving to go deep enough in daily praying to graduate from the peewee league.

## A Good Defense

Many problems have a spiritual root and are best addressed in the spiritual realm. Ephesians 6:12 reminds us that "our struggle is not against flesh and blood." When troubles are deep-seated and long-standing, try kneeling!

Countless conflicts could be resolved simply if we would humble ourselves and pray (2 Chron. 7:14). The primary reason we see so few prayer victories is because we engage in so few prayer battles. Our spiritual fight is on the prayer front. We move forward on our knees.

"Prayer warfare is not your begging God to help you do His will, or trying to convince God of the magnitude of a need," said Wesley Duewel. "Prayer warfare is joining Christ in driving out and defeating Satan and in setting his captives free."[7]

I have experienced spiritual warfare personally. I've struggled with the powers of darkness and prevailed. When we resist the devil, he flees (James 4:7). The one who is in you is greater than the one who is in the world (1 John 4:4).

Never accept spiritual defeat. Stand strong in the fight. We are more than conquerors through him who loved us (Rom. 8:37). Prevailing prayer is our best defense against the world, the flesh, and the devil.

## Prayer Is Listening

God desires to speak to us, but we must be open to hear his voice, responding like young Samuel, "Speak, LORD, for your servant is listening" (1 Sam. 3:9).

We may wait for the answer, but never in vain. "When God brings a time of waiting, and appears to be unresponsive, don't fill it with busyness," advised Oswald Chambers, "just wait. The time of waiting may come to teach you the meaning of sanctification."[8]

For most of my life, I've treated God like Santa, offering my wish lists and hoping he will come through on at least some of them. I'm not the only one who's done that. Occasionally, overzealous ministers make arrogant "God owes you one" claims. "If you have enough faith, you can make him do whatever you want." But who are we to boss God around? Isn't it foolish of us to tell him what to do? That's sort of like the flea thinking he owns the dog.

Now, of course, our Lord invites us to bring all our burdens to him. He desires to help us carry the heavy load. However, it's not our job to manipulate him into fulfilling our desires. Rather, our aim in prayer should be to discover what he wants and then do it.

## Two Ways to Pray God's Will

Here are two suggestions to align your prayers to God's will.

### Pray the Scriptures

God's Word is always his will. Praying Scripture over your family, friends, church, and into your present situation is certainly in line with his loving heart.

### Ask God for His Prayer List

Quietly ask God to bring to your mind who you should lift up in prayer, then wait. Names of different people, nations, or groups will come to you. God is revealing them to you so you can bless them by lifting them back to him.

## Prayer Is Lifting

When we pray for others, it brings real strength to them. We are, after all, called to "carry each other's burdens" (Gal. 6:2) and a primary way to do this is through intercessory prayer. We truly can lift up each other to the throne of grace.

One of the best things I've ever done for my congregation is to start praying for them by name. For many years, I prayed for them in the broad, general sense: "Dear God, bless all the people in my church." Of course, there would be special prayer needs that would come along, but for the most part, it was hit and miss. In fact, there were several members who I had never once prayed for specifically. People would often come to me with prayer requests, and I would always agree to remember them. But sometimes I forgot until I saw them again. Then I would shoot a quick prayer up, "Lord, please retro this prayer back to Tuesday when they really needed it!"

But a few years ago, I learned how to actively engage in prayer for the members of my flock. I try to pray for them all by name every week. I don't always make it, but that's my goal. There are several pages of names. Sometimes, I pray quickly through the list. Then, God will prompt me to stop and linger on behalf of an individual or family. Often, I later learn of a special need they had right when I was praying for them. Also, praying through the list helps me keep my word. When I tell people I will pray for them, I really will. When I see their name, I automatically remember their request. This practice also helps me remember names better. When I see Josh and Sally come in with their son, I know his name is Justin because I prayed for him on Tuesday.

## A Powerful Prayer Pattern

The following pattern has proven helpful in strengthening my prayer life.

### Focus

Tune your mind and heart to God—his greatness, depth, love, and grace. What about distractions? Here's an idea: capture the distracting thoughts and turn them into prayers. Writing prayers is another way to deal with distractions. You won't go on rabbit trails nearly so much when you're writing.

### Faith

Recognizing God's mighty power infuses prayer with faith. A great way to express faith while praying is to start with "thank you" rather than "please."

### Forgiveness

Search your heart. Ask God to cleanse all sin and heal your brokenness. Open your heart to forgive those who have wronged you. You cannot have power in prayer and unforgiveness too.

### Filling

Seek the fullness of the Holy Spirit. Don't just ask for things; ask for him. Don't just ask him to come through for you; ask him to come. A one-word biblical prayer is *Maranatha*, meaning "Come, Lord Jesus."

### Flowing

Prepare your heart to go and bless others, bringing hope, encouragement, and holy love. "Flow through me, Lord. Flow through me."

## Your Prayer List

When my father died, we found several lists of names tucked in his Bible. They were the people he lifted to the Lord daily. It is helpful to have tools to remember others in prayer.

Here are a few good places to find a prayer list:

- Your cell phone contacts. Scroll through and pray for each one.
- Your Facebook friends.
- Billboards. As you're driving, use billboards as prayer springboards. If you're creative, each one will prompt you to pray for somebody.
- ABC's. Go through the alphabet, praying for two or three people per letter.

In her last years, my prayer partner, Judy, suffered from a broken hip and was confined to a rehabilitation center far from home. On Maundy Thursday, I brought her Communion.

"How are you today, Judy?"

"Oh, just wonderful," she replied, "I've been all over the world this morning. I've travelled to Nepal, North Korea, Japan, and Haiti."

I marveled at Judy's adventurous attitude. Here she was, suffering in a strange place and unable to walk, yet a world traveller through her intercession.


## Amen and Amen

Contrary to popular understanding, the word *amen* does not end a prayer, but is the trigger that shoots it out: "So be it!"

Any prayer of faith birthed in God's heart and breathed according to his will is eternal. It never ends. My father's prayers are still going strong, even though he died over two decades ago. My prayers join the grand symphony of the saints that will continue throughout the ages. Prayer power compounds.

Amen and Amen!

PART 3

# Fluo

to flow, pour, stream

Whoever believes in me, as the Scripture has said,
streams of living water will flow from within him.

—John 7:38

Dear friends, since God so loved us,
we also ought to love one another.
—1 John 4:11

# 9

# Compassion
## Pour Out God's Presence

Compassion is love in action—what we do to benefit others. If your heart is full of Jesus, it will naturally overflow with love. Your discipleship, then, is measured by the depth and width of your love.

Those who major in legalistic religion often fail the final exam. If you miss love, you flunk the course. Compassion is a vital sign of spirituality. Disregarding others reveals ungodliness, regardless of how much holy talk or Christian speak you use (1 John 4:20).

## Compass

The first seven letters in the word *compassion* spell "compass." A compass is an instrument that points to true north and gets you out of the woods.

## True North

When my friend Todd took me hunting deep in the wilderness, he pinned a compass on my collar and said, "Follow this straight west to find the truck." He then boosted me up a tree and left.

Chilled to the bone and bored stiff after hours of fruitless tree sitting, I called it quits. Clumsily, I climbed down, took a gander at the compass, and headed west. Unfortunately, I didn't realize the folded knife in my front pocket drew the compass off center, so I walked in circles. I'd probably still be out there circumnavigating if Todd hadn't tracked me down.

Christ's love is our true north, and compassion means following it in the right direction. Sometimes we unwittingly allow other things to draw us from that path.

## Circle Making

A compass is also a simple tool used to make excellent circles. When I draw circles freehand, they look like kidney beans. But a compass considerably improves my circle-making ability.

You can't use love as a compass without drawing a wide circle. Ingrown churches misunderstand this important principle. Ask them to describe themselves, and you'll hear such adjectives as *warm* and *caring*. However, their small circles are turned inward with the warmth and care shared only with each other. Outside they've posted "No Trespassing" for intruders.

Holy huddles dishonor God. Compassion calls us to push the circle wider than our easy, little fellowship of family and friends. It even urges us to encircle those who have shut us out.

Edwin Markham, responding to such rejection, said,

He drew a circle that shut me out—
Heretic, rebel, a thing to flout.

But Love and I had the wit to win:
We drew a circle that took him in![1]

## Facing the Wrong Direction

In a defining moment for Hayward Wesleyan Church, my carpenter friend, Nate Yoder, reminded us to keep our circle wide when we dedicated our new property. We had outgrown our building, and about twenty of us met on our new land for a prayer of blessing and dedication. We made a circle, held hands, and I was just about to commence, when Nate interrupted, "Wait! We're facing the wrong direction. Shouldn't we be facing out toward the community rather than looking at each other? Aren't we doing this for the people who haven't come yet?"

Convicted of our inward posture, we all immediately agreed, turned around, and prayed a different kind of dedication and blessing. We dedicated ourselves to Christ and asked him to use us to bring blessing to the whole community.

## Encompassed

The word *encompass* means to encircle completely. Just as a mountain encompasses a lake and a ring encompasses a finger, so God's love surrounds everything completely. You can't go any place where his love hasn't already gone. It's a love beyond imagination or compare.

"And I pray that you, being rooted and established in love, may have power, together with all the saints, to grasp how wide and long and high and deep is the love of Christ, and to know this love that surpasses knowledge—that you may be filled to the measure of all the fullness of God" (Eph. 3:17–19).

On his deathbed, John Fletcher captured a glimpse of love's reality. His wife reported: "On Wednesday . . . he told me, he had received such a manifestation of the full meaning of that word, *God is love*, as he could never be able to tell. *It fills me*, said he; it *fills me* every moment. O Polly! My dear Polly! *God is love!* Shout, shout aloud, O! It so fills me, I want a gust of praise to go to the ends of the earth."[2] His last words, attempting to describe this holy love, were, "Boundless! Boundless!"

Encompassed by such boundless love, we are empowered to freely love others.

## Love God

Jesus said the greatest commandment is to love God with all our hearts, souls, minds, and strength (Mark 12:30). Loving God is the essence of true spirituality and our highest calling.

Christians of every tribe believe it, but we often fall short moving it from creed to deed. We must love, not just with words, but also with actions (1 John 3:18). Mark Batterson says, "The rallying cry of the next reformation is *'Amo Dei.'* Translation: 'Love God.'"[3] Sign me up for the reformation! I'll help hammer this note on the cathedral door. Loving God is not an option, but a command.

But this brings us to a perplexing dilemma. How can love possibly be commanded? If it has to be commanded, is it really love? Demanding love pushes people in the opposite direction. "You *have* to love me!" sounds like a desperate boyfriend or the ranting of a conflicted boss. How can it truly be love if it's forced? Isn't love always a gift?

The only way this command makes sense is if we understand it as the natural response to God's overwhelming love for us. He isn't commanding us to do anything he hasn't already done first. He fills us with his holy love so we can pour it back out. Any love we have is merely a reflection of his. "The love I have for you, my Lord is only a shadow of your love for me; your deep, abiding love."[4]

God first loved us, and we can't help but love him in return (1 John 4:19). If we are called to love God with heart, soul, mind, and strength, isn't it reasonable to believe that he loved us that way first?

Just imagine—almighty God, the great Creator and essence of everything, the ground of all being, and source of all life, fountain of love, center of knowledge, King of Kings, and Lord of Lords loves you! Such love is difficult to comprehend. Like an ocean, you can see its beginning but not its end. Boundless! He loves you with all his heart; no love could possibly reach wider than that. He loves you with all his soul; no love could possibly go deeper than that. He loves you with all his mind; no love could possibly have more meaning than that. He loves you with all his strength; no love could possibly be more powerful than that.

When we grasp the immensity of this love, so generously lavished on us (1 John 3:1), we can't help but love him with all our hearts, souls, minds, and strength in return. He loved us that way first—so we automatically love him that way back. No other option makes sense.

"The aim of God in history," noted Dallas Willard, "is the creation of an all-inclusive community of loving persons, with Himself included in that community as its primary sustainer and most glorious inhabitant."[5]

John Wesley expressed this concept in his sermon "The Character of a Methodist":

A Methodist is . . . one who "loves the Lord his God with all his heart, and with all his soul, and with all his mind, and with all his strength." God is the joy of his heart, and the desire of his soul; which is constantly crying out, "Whom have I in heaven but thee? And there is none upon earth that I desire besides thee! My God and my all! Thou art the strength of my heart, and my portion for ever. He is therefore happy in God, yea, always happy, as having in him "a well of water springing up into everlasting life," and overflowing his soul with peace and joy."[6]

Holiness is a singleness of intent (loving God) with a broadness of spirit (loving others.)

## Love Your Neighbor

Love your neighbor as yourself. A Christ-filled heart naturally pours itself out in compassionate care for others. This is missional holiness. Jesus, of course, is our perfect example of this. He walked in complete love, and the journey led him to lost, broken, and hurting people.

Every time the Bible speaks of Jesus having compassion, it is followed by an act of loving-kindness (see Matt. 14:14; 15:32; 20:34; Mark 1:41; 6:34). In other words, Jesus was *moved* with compassion. For him, it was not just a feeling of pity or sympathy, but a call to do something.

Holy love calls us to pour out our lives for others as an act of worship. "I am already being poured out like a drink offering" (2 Tim. 4:6).

"Compassion is the ultimate apologetic," Mark Batterson observed. "There is no defense against it."[7] They will know we are Christians by our love.

# Who Is My Neighbor?

We love our neighbors from the overflow of Christ's compassion toward us. Who is your neighbor? Anyone whose life intersects yours.

Maybe you should start with your nearest neighbor—your companion. This is the person you are at home with; the one who watches television with you, laughs with you, or shares your bed. This person knows you best and is most often taken for granted.

Practically speaking, what does it mean for you to love your nearest neighbor as yourself? How about your children, the folks who live next door, your boss, your enemy, your coworker, those who suffer most in your community, or those who live in other lands? How can you love them as yourself? What adjustments does such love require of you?

The need may be overwhelming, but that is no excuse for doing nothing. Do something for somebody! "Do for one what you wish you could do for everyone."[8]

Listening and lifting are two primary ways to demonstrate compassionate love.

## Love Is in the Listening

You and I have been given two ears and one mouth. That's because we're supposed to listen twice as much as we speak; but talking and explaining come easier than hearing and understanding.

Why is it so hard to listen? Consider this: We speak at 100 to 150 words per minute. We are able to comprehend at 250 to 300 words per minute. We think at 600 words per minute. So, if you are a fast thinker (600 wpm) and the other person is a slow talker (100 wpm), you still have 500 words per minute left over for thinking about other stuff. For efficient folks, that's a lot of wasted communication space.

Therefore, the fast listener tends to zone out and think about a myriad of other things. Zoning out is evidenced by such responses: "Um-hmm," "Yes, dear," "I don't know," and "Whatever." Listening is hard work.

True listening is more than hearing the words. It's processing those words and seeking to understand their depth and meaning. As Jim Elliot journaled, "Wherever you are, be all there."[9] Margaret Wheatley said, "Listening is such a simple act. It requires us to be present, and that takes practice, but we don't have to do anything else. We don't have to advise, or coach, or sound wise. We just have to be willing to sit there and listen."[10]

"Momma, are you listening to me?" little Heidi wondered. "Um-hmm," the distracted mother replied. "No, Momma, I need you to listen with your eyes!"

**Hard of Listening.** Lately, my family has been making fun of my hearing loss. I make them repeat everything and then accuse them of mumbling. It's my price for blaring Bob Dylan through headphones as a teenager. Since I can't hear as well these days, I'm trying to listen better.

Being hard of hearing is not nearly as bad as hard of listening.

Christians have a reputation of being hard of listening. As Rick Warren noted, "For some time now, the hands and feet of the body of Christ have been amputated, and we've been pretty much reduced to a big mouth."[11]

**Listening Point.** Sigurd Olson, the Northwoods naturalist, affectionately dubbed his wilderness cabin on northern Minnesota's Burntside Lake, "Listening Point." Sig explained, "I named this place Listening Point because only when one comes to listen, only when one is aware and still, can things be seen and heard."[12]

Can you imagine how rich our relationships would be if we approached them all as listening points?

Every person, after all, has a fascinating story. Dave Isay, the founder of StoryCorps, discovered this traveling across America in the daunting task of archiving the nation's oral history. He recorded over ten thousand personal stories and concluded, "Listening is an act of love."[13]

## Love Is in the Lifting

Shortly after the devastating January 2010 Haiti earthquake, Dr. Jo Anne Lyon related the following story.

An orphanage near the epicenter that housed 131 children was flattened. Rescue workers found 130 children, but there was one little girl still missing. They searched through the night, and finally found her the next morning, trapped in a small space with barely enough room to breathe. After they dug her from the rubble, they asked, "Charity, what did you do while you were trapped there all those hours?

To this, she replied, "I sang, 'Love lifted me. Love lifted me. When nothing else could help, love lifted me.'"[14]

That is exactly what happened. The loving hands of God's people reached out and lifted that precious little girl. This is missional holiness. Holy love lifts the load. It goes the extra mile. If we say we love but are not willing to lift, we're just posers.

A guy boasted on his Facebook status, "I have over a thousand friends!" To this, someone commented, "And how many of them would help you move a piano?" Heavy hefting proves true friendship. Love is in the lifting.

Love lifts, but there's an amazing twist to it: the more you love, the lighter the load. The burden doesn't seem nearly so heavy when the lifting is a labor of love.

## Love Is the Work of the Church

If we're not careful, church business can get in the way of the church's real business. The story of the good Samaritan demonstrates this vividly. The priest and Levite who passed by the battered traveler on the road were too busy to care. They were so preoccupied with "serving God" that they failed to stop and serve him. Though the psalmist rightly exalts clean hands and a pure heart, these guys would have done better if they had paused and dirtied their hands.

Sharon Rhodes Wickett in her powerful sermon, "Collapsing the Distance between Heaven and Earth," related the following incident:

I attended the annual conference of the Methodist Church in Sierra Leone, West Africa. The meetings were held in the large sanctuary in the capital city, Freetown.

Each day as we entered the large doors into the sanctuary, there was a young girl, maybe about the age of eight, who begged at the door. She looked ragged, dirty; her hair was matted and knotty; and she had on tattered clothes. No one seemed to know her, and people brushed her aside upon entering. Some of the pastors tried to tell her to go away. We were busy doing the work of the church; she was a bother. This went on for several days.

As I sat in the pew observing the conference one day, my peripheral vision caught some motion outside. I looked out the window, and there on the patio, outside the sanctuary was a woman, a lay member of the conference. She found a bucket and some soap. Although dressed in a beautiful traditional tie-dye gown, she pushed up her sleeves, and she was giving that eight-year-old girl a bath. She soaped up her hair and was tenderly making her all clean and new. She washed the clothes the child had been wearing, and they were spread out on the bushes in the sun drying. The woman went out and got another dress for her to wear too.

Hundreds of pastors and devoted lay persons poured into the Methodist Church of Freetown to do the work of the church. But outside, on the edges, quietly and without notice, the work of redemption—the work of Jesus Christ was being done. It was not the work of committees and reports and programs. It was the work of soap and water and human touch and being able to see the face of Jesus in that of an abandoned child.[15]

Jesus said, "Greater love has no one than this, that he lay down his life for his friends" (John 15:13).

The Word became flesh and made his dwelling among us.
We have seen his glory, the glory of the One and Only,
who came from the Father, full of grace and truth.

—John 1:14

# 10

# Blessing
## Pour Out God's Promise

"Lord, make me a blessing" is a prayer God almost always answers with "Yes!" He longs to pour out blessings through those who willingly make themselves available. Availability after all is the greatest ability required to share holy love with others.

Everyone you meet carries a burden and needs a blessing. If you have eyes to see and ears to hear, you will notice. But most of us are too focused on ourselves to pay attention. Faith is being filled with God's promise, and blessing is pouring it out with grace and truth.

## Way to Go, Graceful!

Raised in an old-fashioned holiness parsonage, I learned a lot about Jesus, but there were certain childhood deprivations. "Shunning the appearance of evil," we never wore shorts, played cards, swam with the opposite sex, went to movies, bowled, or roller skated.

During my high school rebellion, I went to the beach a few times and snuck off to the movies to watch the original *Star Wars*. Somewhere between galactic battles and fistfuls of popcorn, I imagined Jesus returning before the film ended, leaving me behind with a room full of sci-fi pagans. Fortunately, Jesus held off long enough for me to finish the show.

During my adolescent oat sowing, one sin I never committed was roller skating. "Skating is dancing on wheels!" Daddy thundered from the pulpit, and I said, "Amen!" It's one thing to sit in a darkened theater; it's quite another to make a silly spectacle of oneself. I opposed any sin that would make me look stupid.

Then, during my third week as an Indiana Wesleyan University[1] freshman, I was led into temptation. The sophomore class advertised a skating party.

Furthermore, Cathy, the beautiful young lady who sparked my interest (and later became my bride), expressed a desire to attend this event with me. Reluctantly, I agreed, hoping that she'd rather not skate, but sit with me on the sidelines for good Christian fellowship. I prayed, "Please Jesus, help me fade into the background and survive this thing without looking like a complete idiot!" Sometimes Jesus says yes to our prayers; sometimes he says no. This time he said no.

To my horror, the announcer boomed, "Ladies and gentlemen, to begin this evening, let's have all the newly elected class officers come out onto the rink and take a victory lap so we can congratulate you." If I had known this was a part of the package, I never would have permitted my name to be on the ballot for vice president of the freshman class. There was no escape.

As awkward as a skating cow, I stumbled onto the floor, where, to the amusement of the crowd, I demonstrated my complete lack of coordination. Fortunately, Cathy had been elected too. So, clasping my hand in hers, she held me up with as much dignity as she could muster.

As we finished the lap together, my roommate shouted encouragement, "Way to go, graceful!" I thought he was talking to me. Reflecting back, however, I think maybe he must have meant Cathy. It took extraordinary grace for her to bear this humiliation, and she didn't even seem to mind. Although, come to think of it, she hasn't asked me to go skating for at least twenty-five years.

The word *graceful* means "full of grace." That's the best word I can use to describe Cathy. Through our decades together since that awkward skating debut, she has demonstrated grace upon grace, reflecting the holy love she has embraced for herself. Cathy is also full of truth. She gently chides me when I exaggerate or adjust the facts to fit my stories. The right mix of grace and truth makes her lovely, rock solid, and a blessing to everyone who knows her. "Hail Cathy, full of grace, the Lord is with thee."

## The Purple Grace-Truth Blend

The only way to genuinely bless others is through a humble spirit of grace and truth. Without either quality, it doesn't feel like much of a blessing. A blessing isn't really a blessing unless the person on the receiving end experiences it that way.

Not everyone who comes to help is helpful; they just think they are. Self-promotion disguised as compassion leads to resentment rather than genuine blessing. Humble, graceful truth is the key that unlocks the blessing door.

Without the truth, we're insincere. Without the grace, we're irritating. We must be filled with both to bless.

If truth is red and grace is blue, our interactions and conversations should be purple and marked by a blending of the following:

- Charity and Clarity: Don't muddle truth for kindness, but speak it clearly with love.
- Appreciation and Sincerity: Express honest gratitude without leaving false impressions.
- Generosity and Expectancy: Give grace freely, but understand the necessity of expecting and evaluating results.
- Respect and Security: Treat everyone with equal respect, remembering "God does not show favoritism" (Acts 10:34). We need self-respect (inner security) in order to respect others appropriately.

## Truth without Grace

Some people maximize truth and minimize grace. I've met plenty of church leaders who fit that description. In an unwavering quest for truth, they leave a wide swath of unnecessary carnage. Sometimes I agree with what they're saying but disagree with how they're saying it. A friend once asked, "Why is it that the people I agree with are hardest to like?"

"It's the shrill tone," I replied. "I think they're just tone deaf."

Of course, "nothing but the truth" tellers bring a necessary prophetic perspective to the church. In our day of diluted discipleship, we need a clear voice of challenge and rebuke. However, truth untempered by grace comes off as harsh judgmentalism or cold cynicism. You cannot bless others when your spirit is icy and negative.

## Grace without Truth

On the other hand, people pleasers maximize grace and minimize truth.

Did you hear about the insecure doctor who wanted everybody to like him? He only told patients what they wanted to hear and is facing multiple malpractice suits. We expect physicians to be honest, even if it's bad news.

Spiritual healing occurs only after truthful diagnosis. "Behold, I will bring it health and cure, and I will cure them, and will reveal unto them the abundance of peace and truth" (Jer. 33:6 KJV).

Regrettably, many church leaders are afraid to speak up because they don't want to offend anybody. When it comes to truth telling, silence is not golden but plain yellow.

Jesus always spoke candidly, and we should follow his example of stating the truth in love. "Let your conversation be always full of grace, seasoned with salt, so that you may know how to answer everyone" (Col. 4:6).

## Blessed to Bless

Blessing means bestowing favor or well-being. It is a grand scriptural theme, with over four hundred references. At the beginning of Genesis, the first thing God did after making people was bless them (Gen. 1:27–28). The Bible ends with a blessing as well (Rev. 22:21). So from beginning to end and all through the middle, the Lord brings blessings.

God's relationship with his people has always been based on covenant that includes a promise and blessing for those who choose to live in it. Old Testament heroes Adam, Noah, Abraham, Moses, and David all received a special promise and blessing based on faith. In the New Testament, Jesus brought promise and blessing even more powerfully through the Holy Spirit. "He redeemed us in order that the blessing given to Abraham might come to the Gentiles through Christ Jesus, so that by faith we might receive the promise of the Spirit (Gal. 3:14).

God told Abraham that he was blessed to be a blessing (Gen. 12:2). And this is true for you. If you have been blessed, it's not just for your own consumption. God blesses people so they can bless others. That's the essence of sharing your faith—simply pouring out the blessing of love you have received. Brian Lusky captured this thought beautifully in a song: "You're the overflow, the sustainer of my soul. Flowing out of me, living water for the weary."[2]

## Treasure Hunt

I teach evangelism classes for ministerial students, and as a part of the course, we spend an afternoon out in the community sharing our faith. When I announce this excursion, most students aren't too thrilled about the prospect. They anxiously imagine going door-to-door or blasting bullhorns. I smile, recalling Rebecca Pippert's observation, "Christians and non-Christians have something in common: We're both uptight about evangelism."[3]

Then I explain that our faith-sharing experience is not about haranguing, arguing, or pressuring people into conversion. Instead, it's an experiment in loving and blessing. I call it the treasure hunt.

"God is going to lead you to someone he treasures—someone who needs encouragement," I tell them, "and your task is to simply follow the Spirit's promptings, so you can discover them and remind them how deeply they're loved."

Then after some prayerful reflection, we go out to bless people. This approach works! Every time, my students return bubbling over with thrilling stories of divine appointments and powerful prayer encounters.

When we humbly ask the Lord to make us a blessing, he gladly takes us up on the offer.

## Shooting Blessings

Driving down Main Street with my little girl in the back seat, I glanced in the rearview mirror and caught her aiming a finger gun at unsuspecting pedestrians. "Pow! Pow! Pow!"

"Hannah, cut that out!" I scolded. "It's not nice. We don't shoot people; we bless them."

After riding in silence for a few minutes, she started up again— this time with two fingers, "Pow! Pow! Pow!"

"Hannah, didn't I tell you to stop shooting people?"

"But Daddy," she replied, "this time, I'm shooting blessings!"

Shooting blessings requires a few essentials.

### Positive Energy

Some folks run on positive juice, and others run on negative. Likewise, some churches operate with positive energy while others function in the negative. You can actually grow a congregation using either kind of energy, but they will have very different atmospheres.

Negative energy churches attract sour, pessimistic people who thrive on conflict and melodrama. Positive energy churches, on the other hand, draw hopeful, visionary optimists. Which kind of people do you want to attract?

### Encouraging Words

Everyone is imperfect, but we must look for the good rather than finding fault. Building up others is called edification, and this begins at home. Are you speaking your most encouraging words to those closest to you?

In a wedding ceremony, I meant to say "build each other up," while impressing the importance of edification in marriage. Instead I slipped and said, "So, don't tear each other down. Tear each other up." I hope they didn't take me up on that one. Too many couples tear each other up with hurtful words.

We all need encouragement, but that won't come in families or congregations bent on devouring one another. Focus on the good in each other and in the church.

Driving home from church, a family hashed over the worship service. "The sermon was boring." "The drums were too loud." "The soloist sang off key." Then, little Jimmy piped up, "But I don't think it was such a bad show for a dollar."

## Common Ground

We are all made of the same stuff. An attitude of superiority is easily detected and alienates us from others. We must remember that we are no better than anybody else.

For years, Jim Bob regularly called me requesting financial assistance, and it began to wear thin. One morning our secretary, Donna, buzzed me. "Jim Bob's on the phone again. Do you want to talk to him?"

"No!" I responded. "I really don't want to talk to him, but now that he's on hold waiting for me, I guess I have to."

In the seconds between my response and picking up the receiver, the Holy Spirit convicted me: "Jim Bob is precious to me. I love him just as much as I love you, and you need to treat him with respect, as your equal."

"Lord, forgive me," I prayed. "Help me to see Jim Bob through your eyes." Then I picked up the phone.

"Guess what, Pastor Mark?" Jim Bob exuded. "I'm over at the hospital. My daughter just had a baby boy, and I wanted you to be the first to know!"

Chastened, I hung up after the congratulations, went directly to Donna, and apologized. "I was totally wrong in the way I responded. I should never have treated Jim Bob with such disrespect."

Donna smiled.

## Mission Enlistment

One of the best ways to bless people is to enlist them in service for others. My friend Ruth Tucker has noted that inviting unbelieving friends to join you in serving others is a tremendous way to introduce them to Christ. She calls it friendship evangelism in reverse.[4]

Our church board invited a group of twentysomethings to the meeting for a special listening session. "We would like to see you guys more involved in the life of the church," we said. "What can we do for you?"

Josh, a bright emerging leader said, "That's exactly the problem. We don't want you to do things for us. We want you to do things with us. If you're going to do something to serve others, invite us along. We would be honored to help."

## The Big Yes Bias

Effective spiritual leaders have a bias for the big yes. "For no matter how many promises God has made, they are 'Yes' in Christ" (2 Cor. 1:20).

I am not advocating a yes to every request or idea that comes along. Excellence means saying no to lesser things in order to say yes to the best. This requires turning down most good ideas and all the bad ones. Every communication, however, includes two communications: what you are saying and whether you care.

When it comes to blessing people, we should always have a "Yes, I care about you" attitude, and every *no* must be spoken within the context of the bigger *yes*. The art of gracious refusal is a valuable skill every minister must learn.

Our family has been involved in Bible quizzing for years. We've noticed in competitions that some quiz masters seem to be for the quizzers while others seem to be against them. The "for the quizzer" officials have a better grasp of their mission and a greater rapport with the participants.

How you treat others is more important than just about anything else. Poet Maya Angelou said, "People will forget what you said, people will forget what you did, but people will never forget how you made them feel."[5]

## Blessing and Belonging

Blessing brings belonging. When a person feels blessed, they also feel accepted.

*The Blessing* by Gary Smalley and John Trent shares five ways to bless loved ones and convey a deep sense of inclusion:

- meaningful touch,
- words of encouragement,
- attaching high value,
- picturing a special future, and
- active commitment.[6]

Countless homes have been enriched by Smalley and Trent's insights. But too often we leave the blessing at home. What would happen if Christian leaders took these blessing practices out of the house? What if we treated everybody like this? What if we viewed ourselves as blessing bringers, reaching out and widening our circle of belonging?

Can you imagine the difference it would make if we committed ourselves to intentionally blessing those on the fringes of the congregation and community through meaningful touch, words of encouragement, attaching high value, and picturing a special future?

Many people, especially young adults, feel excluded. Sociologist Christian Smith, researching emerging adult spirituality, discovered that most young people (even those who regularly attend) do not feel a sense of belonging at church.[7] Perhaps this is because the church has not been deliberate enough in bringing blessing to them through meaningful relationships. Belonging is blessing's fruit. If you want people to feel included and accepted, start blessing them.

## Blessing Others

Salvation Army founder William Booth is said to have sent a Christmas telegram to Salvationists around the world. Funds were tight so the message was concise: "Others!"

Who are the "others" we are called to bless?

### Bless Those Who Love You

Begin at home. Is the gospel you profess good news to your family? Do they feel cherished and valued? How can you bring them joy?

### Bless Those Who Lead You

The troops tend to gripe. Has your spirit been critical toward the person in charge? Are you aware of the load this person is carrying? What can you do to help?

### Bless Those Who Help You

Do you take the people who serve beside you for granted? Are you using them to further your own agenda? Do you know what's going on in their hearts and lives? What can you do to encourage them?

### Bless Those Who Disappoint You

When people fail, how do you treat them? Are you gracious toward those who let you down, giving them another chance without reluctance?

### Bless Those Who Dislike You

Jesus specifically told us to bless and pray for those who curse us (Luke 6:28). Are you blessing your enemies? It's hard to hold a grudge against someone you're praying for.

## Stay in the Grace Bubble and Bless Everybody

Timber Tina is a professional lumberjack sports athlete. She was the national logrolling champion and runs summertime lumberjack shows in Maine as well as exhibitions across the country. Her pickup truck sports a bumper sticker that reads, "Beware of Chicks with Axes." Folks don't mess with Timber Tina!

It was a great joy for me to help Tina discover a deep and personal faith to accompany her zest for life. I could tell that Tina had something important on her mind one spring morning when she stepped into my office.

"Pastor Mark," she began, "you are sworn to secrecy."

Remembering her bumper sticker, I immediately agreed to keep my lips sealed.

"I've landed a spot on the *Survivor* television program and am heading to Guatemala next week."

"Wow, Tina! That's wonderful! I hope you win a million bucks."

"It's just an honor to be selected," she replied. "But I came here to ask if you would pray for me and for my son Charlie while I am away."

"Of course Tina. I'll pray for you both every day while you're there."

I gave her a hug with my blessing and a pocket camouflage adventure Bible, and she left for Maine to get her lumberjack show staff ready before heading to Guatemala.

The next Saturday evening, I received a heart-wrenching telephone call from Hayward Memorial Hospital. Charlie, Tina's sixteen-year-old son, had just been killed in a car accident. I couldn't believe it. Charlie was such a wonderful young man full of joy and vigor. How could he possibly be gone? Shocked, I immediately went to comfort his friends and family who gathered in the emergency room.

Calling Tina in Maine about the accident was one of the hardest things I have ever done. She was absolutely devastated. Tina rushed home as quickly as possible, and we walked into the funeral parlor together. *Survivor* was now more than a television role to Tina. It was the very theme of her life. How could she possibly survive this terrible ordeal?

As the youth group worship team sang "I Can Only Imagine" at Charlie's funeral, we all sensed an outpouring of divine love and peace. I was reminded that saving grace is keeping grace, and the God of the mountain is also the God of the valley.

In the following weeks, I prayed often for Tina, that God would bring her daily help and strength.

One afternoon several months later, Tina called again. "The *Survivor* people contacted me again and asked if I could go on the next show. I think I should do it for Charlie. He was my biggest supporter the first time, and I know he would want me to try."

"Go for it, Tina," I answered. "And I hope you win a million bucks."

Once again, Tina packed her bags, this time to Panama, to compete for the elusive prize.

Tina was silent in the weeks following her return home. She didn't tell anybody how she fared, and none of us dared to ask.

Then the day of the season's premiere, Tina called me. "I need to discuss something really important with you."

My heart leaped. I figured the only reason why she urgently needed to talk with me before the program aired was because she had won the grand prize. I began daydreaming about the building program we would launch after she made a big donation to the church.

Tina arrived at my office and, after making sure nobody else was listening, whispered, "They voted me off the island first."

My grandiose plans for a sanctuary expansion evaporated immediately.

"Everybody in town is wishing me well, pumping me for information, and assuming since I'm not saying anything that I'm the big winner. Tonight the whole world is going to watch me get voted off the island. My friends are going to be so disappointed."

"Yeah, I understand that," I commiserated.

"But the worst part is that I have to fly to New York and appear on *The Early Show*. That makes me so nervous that I think I might faint or throw up right there on national TV. What if I say something stupid? I'm petrified! Will you pray for me?"

I agreed, of course, and just then an idea sparked. It was one of those special God thoughts. "Tina, I know what you need to do. Just picture yourself completely surrounded by a big bubble of grace: above you, beneath you, before you, behind you. As long as you stay in the grace bubble, you will be completely safe. You are with God, and he is with you. Nothing can harm you. My suggestion to you Tina is to stay in the bubble and bless everybody."

She didn't seem convinced but promised to give it a try.

That night, all of Hayward watched Timber Tina light the fire, build the shelter, lead her team in prayer, and catch a fish with her bare hands. She was clearly the strongest competitor of the group. Then at the show's conclusion, the tribe voted her off the island.

The next morning, I tuned in to *The Early Show* and watched Tina handle the interview masterfully. She even put in a good plug about life's highest priorities and told the world about Charlie. I couldn't have been more proud to be her pastor and friend.

A couple of days after her return, she came to see me again. "It worked!" she exclaimed. "I stayed in the bubble and blessed everybody. I blessed the limousine driver who picked me up at the airport. I blessed the doorman at the hotel. I blessed the lady at the front desk. I blessed the whole crew and the anchors on the set, and then, when the cameras started rolling, I thought, "And God bless America!'"

"And God bless you too Tina," I said. "God bless you too."

Peacemakers who sow in peace raise
a harvest of righteousness.

—James 3:18

# 11

# Righteousness

## Pour Out God's Peace

Contentment is being filled with God's peace, and we pour it out through righteousness. The prophet Isaiah declared, "Justice will dwell in the desert and righteousness live in the fertile field. The fruit of righteousness will be peace; the effect of righteousness will be quietness and confidence forever" (Isa. 32:16–17).

## What Righteousness Isn't

What does peacemaking righteousness look like? Perhaps the best approach is to identify what it isn't.

## Not Rule Righteousness

Christ's righteousness is not about vain rule keeping. It isn't about trying harder to be nice instead of naughty. Many believers mistakenly assume spiritual maturity is about striving to be a good boy or girl.

That's about the same level of righteousness achieved by our beloved dog, Vin. He longs for "good boy" status, but often makes messes then resorts to forlorn eyes until we let him out of the doghouse.

If anybody attained righteousness by being good boys, it would have been young John Wesley and his Oxford Holy Club buddies. Along with his brother Charles, George Whitefield, and other students, this little band of zealots followed a strict program of rising early for prayer, fasting twice a week, holding accountability sessions, aiding the poor, and visiting the sick. In many ways, they were the type most churches would love to have leading their young adult ministries.

They proudly bore the scorn of contemporaries who considered them odd, throwing such insults as "Bible bigots," "Bible moths," and "Methodists." One bemused bard quipped: "By rule they eat, by rule they drink, by rule they do all things but think."[1]

Disregarding public opinion, they pressed on the upward way. But something rang hollow in John Wesley's soul. Although he was doing right things and good deeds, his relationship with God was neither right nor good. There was no peace.

After a disastrous stint as an unsuccessful missionary in Savannah, Wesley was forced to face the ugly truth. He saw himself as he really was: an over-religious, overcontrolling, overphilosophizing sinner desperately in need of saving grace. Perhaps Solomon had someone like Wesley in mind when he wrote, "Do not be overrighteous" (Eccl. 7:16).

At 8:45 p.m. on May 24, 1738, at a small Moravian gathering on Aldersgate Street in London, John Wesley realized the futility of his strivings and embraced grace by faith alone. He wrote, "I felt my heart strangely warmed. I felt I did trust in Christ, Christ alone for salvation: And an assurance was given me, that he had taken away *my* sins, even *mine*, and saved *me* from the law of sin and death."[2]

Later in his sermon "Salvation by Faith," Wesley explained that even righteous acts are "all unholy and sinful themselves, so that every one of them needs a fresh atonement."[3] It was this simple concept of Christ alone as his righteousness that transformed John Wesley's life.

More than twenty years ago, I experienced something similar. I was a youth pastor striving to keep the rules, and did a fairly decent job of it. However, deep in my soul like rule-bound Wesley, I knew I wasn't right with God. I was religious with little glimpses of righteousness. But at 6:15 a.m. on December 6, 1990, everything changed when I knelt in an empty sanctuary, poured out everything to Christ, and asked him to cleanse and fill me completely with holy love.

My spiritual goal immediately changed from being a good boy for Jesus to overflowing with him. What a difference it made!

### Self-Righteousness

The righteousness that brings peace is not the kind we use to justify ourselves with comparisons. It's human nature to deflect attention from our shortcomings to the failures of others. I think this is why gossip is so prevalent. In some twisted way, bad-mouthing someone else makes us feel better about ourselves. Those who look and act righteous sometimes aren't what they seem. "Man looks at the outward appearance, but the LORD looks at the heart" (1 Sam. 16:7).

The most "religious" people in the Bible were the Pharisees. But Jesus repeatedly condemned their self-righteousness. "Unless your righteousness surpasses that of the Pharisees and the teachers of the law, you will certainly not enter the kingdom of heaven" (Matt. 5:20). He wasn't saying we need to be more righteous in the Pharisee way. Instead, he was declaring an entirely different kind of righteousness:

- Humility rather than haughtiness.
- Graciousness rather than harshness.
- Holiness rather than holier-than-thou-ness.

When Christ comes in, he brings his own righteousness with him. We don't need any of our own; he provides it all. He is our righteousness (1 Cor. 1:30). When we're full of Jesus, we're full of righteousness and therefore full of peace. When we're full of self, there is no righteousness, thus no peace.

## Opinion Righteousness

An arrogant guy puffed, "There are two sides to the argument: mine and wrong," proving the adage that some heads, like concrete, are thoroughly mixed up and permanently set. Stiffly opinionated people who disparage all other perspectives miss the larger picture. Not everybody sees things the same way, and after all, we might be mistaken.

Doctrines and beliefs are important, but in the end, Jesus is neither a doctrine nor a belief. He is a living person. Christ calls us to walk in love and cherish him more than our own perspectives.

## True Righteousness

So if the righteousness that brings peace isn't a matter of rule, self, or opinion, then what is it?

- Heart righteousness
- Relationship righteousness
- Holy love righteousness

Beyond beliefs, rituals, and practices, the bigger question is whether your heart harmonizes with God. Being right with him sets us right with others.

The entire Wilson household plays stringed instruments. One evening, we separately tuned our guitars, violin, bass, and viola for a jam session, but when we played together it sounded terrible. Although the instruments were in tune and sounded fine alone, they weren't tuned to each other. It wasn't until we stopped and re-tuned to the master tuner that we were able to make beautiful music together.

The world will find harmony by getting right—one person at a time. But in order to make things right, we must face what's wrong.

## No Unrighteous Peace

If Christ our righteousness is Christ our peace, why did he say "I did not come to bring peace, but a sword" (Matt. 10:34)? Because there is no unrighteous peace.[4]

Sometimes wrongdoing continues unopposed because we don't want to cause trouble and stir a hornets' nest. Under the guise of keeping peace, we tolerate evil and follow the appeasement path.

Confrontation brings conflict, and most of us would rather avoid that at all cost. But there is no unrighteous peace.

The early Wesleyan Methodists understood this. In the mid-1800s, against the popular tide, they vigorously opposed slavery as abolitionists. Countless slaves found liberty through their valiant efforts. Misunderstood and maligned, they suffered severe persecution because they refused to settle for an unrighteous peace.

The old Wesleyan Methodist Church in downtown Syracuse was a major station on the Underground Railroad, smuggling runaway slaves to Canada. They dug a hideout tunnel beneath the church where dozens of fugitives sought refuge every month.

The building still stands, but in recent years has been remodeled as a Mexican restaurant. I had the good fortune to visit a couple of years ago, and since it had just closed, the manager graciously allowed me to descend into the narrow, winding passageway with low ceilings. "The clay and dirt wall of this tunnel bore the human touch of those who had passed through this haven," observed another tunnel pilgrim, Delores Byrnes.[5]

In musty darkness, I was overwhelmed by the significance of this place, the courage of its people, and the conviction of their principles. We cannot fathom the sacrifices these brave souls made for freedom. Perhaps this was the kind of place the psalmist envisioned when he said, "Righteousness and peace have kissed each other" (Ps. 85:10 KJV).

## Adam Crooks

Standing in the slave tunnel, I recalled that funeral services for the great leader Adam Crooks were held in the sanctuary directly above me in 1874.

Decades earlier in October 1847, Crooks, a twenty-three-year-old Buckeye, took the holiness-abolition message deep into slave territory and planted Freedom's Hill Church in Alamance County, North Carolina.[6]

Before departing southward, the young, freshly ordained minister was gripped by a haunting question: "Are you willing to give your life for the cause?"

During his daring Carolina days, Adam Crooks proved this willingness. Though winning many hearts (by promoting holiness), he also made mortal enemies (by promoting abolition) who attacked the congregation and shot at the church. Crooks was tarred in effigy, beaten, poisoned twice, threatened with lynching, dragged from the pulpit, and unjustly imprisoned.

His ministry partner, Jesse McBride, was abused by mobs and arrested. He was also sentenced to twenty lashes on his bare back, the pillory, and jail. He appealed the sentence and left the state before it was carried out. McBride died five years later, a victim of the cruel mistreatment.

Fellow ministers, Jarvis Bacon and Daniel Worth, followed Crooks to North Carolina and imprisonment. A group of thugs captured Micajah McPherson, a leading member of the Freedom's Hill congregation and hung him from a tree in the back field. Miraculously, he survived the hanging.

Why were these men willing to pay such a price? Because they knew there is no such thing as an unrighteous peace.

### Laura Smith Haviland

Pondering these matters in the slave tunnel, I also recalled the unusual story of Laura Smith Haviland. She and her husband, Charles, offered their farm as the first Underground Railroad station in Michigan. Laura also launched the Raisin Institute, the state's first interracial school. She was instrumental in organizing Michigan's first antislavery society.

Tragically widowed at age thirty-six, she cared for her seven children, ran the farm in the face of surmounting debt, led the institute, and continued her antislavery activities.

In 1846 Laura personally travelled to Tennessee in order to free Ellis and Elsie Hamilton's children from their mother's former slave owner, John Chester. The journey turned into a hair-raising misadventure when she was threatened and held at gunpoint. She escaped but was hounded by Chester and his clan for the next fifteen years and was eventually dragged to court for violating the Fugitive Slave Law. All charges were dismissed, but the legal challenges took a tremendous toll.

Why would Laura go to such extremes to help people she did not know? Because it was the right thing to do, and there is no unrighteous peace. Reflecting later she said, "Is it not the duty of every Christian to bring his or her religion into every line of life-work, and act as conscientiously in politics as in church work? Sanctified common sense is loudly called for on the highway of holiness. In whatever condition or station in life we find ourselves, are we not our brother's keeper in a more extensive view than we are prone to conceive?"[7] Today, two American towns are named after Laura Haviland, and her statue graces city hall in Adrian, Michigan.[8]

## From Jeers to Cheers

Jesus said, "Blessed are the peacemakers," and then immediately followed with, "Blessed are those who are persecuted because of righteousness, for theirs is the kingdom of heaven" (Matt. 5:9–10). Peacemaking comes with a price tag.

The abolitionist pioneers willingly paid that price and endured temporary persecution because their eyes were on the greater peace. Time proved them right, and today they are called heroes. In honor of such ardent abolitionists, Rev. Anna Howard Shaw, the first ordained female Methodist, included the following tribute in her autobiography:

They cut a path through tangled underwood
Of old traditions out to broader ways.
They lived to hear their work called brave and good.
But oh! The thorns before the crown of bays.
The world gives lashes to its Pioneers,
Until the goal is reached—then deafening cheers.[9]

Unfortunately, the Wesleyan human rights vanguard lost its steam over the next several decades,[10] and reached a low point on Easter Sunday 1962, when a small group of African-American students visited an Alabama Wesleyan Methodist Church and found they weren't welcome. When the students refused to leave as instructed, someone called the police. Their arrest and removal from the premises received national attention.[11]

## Social Holiness

Over the years reacting to the liberal drift toward a social gospel, the Wesleyans (along with most other evangelicals) divorced personal piety from social concerns and emphasized revival rather than reform. After a few decades, the revival rivers dried up. A church that loses compassion for the poor, lost, and oppressed cannot sustain spiritual revival. Love for God translates into advocacy for others: acting justly, loving mercy, and walking humbly with God (Mic. 6:8).

Heart holiness should always result in a helping hand. When we're right with God, we automatically long to make things right for others.

I am delighted to see a renewed passion in the rising generation to confront the great issues of our day. They are recapturing the heart of John Wesley: "The gospel of Christ knows no religion, but social; no holiness but social holiness."[12]

Although the original context of this specific quote is a rebuttal against "lone ranger religion," there's enough evidence from Wesley's life and writings to also apply it in a larger sense to making the world a better place.

## Social Jesus

Of course, we must keep Jesus as the center of our focus. Misguided passion co-opts Jesus for political purposes. According to Leonard Sweet and Frank Viola, "When 'justice' becomes a goal in itself, or God is equated with justice, then we have moved from Christianity to another religion."[13]

Instead of using Jesus as a means to an end, it should be the other way around. Properly understood, social justice is a great path to Jesus. The church will gain credibility with unbelievers as we become the hands of Christ, reaching out to bless our neighbors and meeting the most pressing needs in the darkest places. In other words: social Jesus!

Righteousness starts on the inside and works outward. Personal holiness translates into social holiness. This is not an either-or proposition, but both-and, like two wings of an airplane, two oars of a rowboat, or two skis.[14]

Holy love stands with the helpless and calls us to address racism, poverty, immorality, inequality, and exploitation.

## Twenty-First-Century Abolition

For instance, there is still a desperate need for abolitionists today. Though slavery is not legal anywhere, it happens everywhere. An estimated twenty-seven million people are involved in some form of modern-day slavery. Two and a half centuries after slavery was essentially abolished worldwide, there are more slaves today than ever before. Victims around the globe are being bought and sold for various exploitative purposes such as forced labor, prostitution, warfare, or forced marriage. This number does not even take into account the estimated 126 million child laborers trapped in hazardous conditions.[15]

Shouldn't twenty-first-century abolitionists be as fervent in their protest as their nineteenth-century predecessors? Shouldn't the church lead the way in freedom's cause? If Christ's followers won't stand against wickedness then who will? What is your part in this fight? There is no unrighteous peace.

On February 2, 2006, Bono, the humanitarian rocker, spoke at the fifty-fourth National Prayer Breakfast in Washington. Although I don't always agree with Bono's pontifications and am more of a bluegrass banjo guy, I thought his comments on behalf of the disenfranchised were profound: "God is with the vulnerable and poor. God is in the slums, in the cardboard boxes where the poor play house . . . God is in the silence of a mother who has infected her child with a virus that will end both their lives . . . God is in the cries heard under the rubble of war . . . God is in the debris of wasted opportunity and lives, and God is with us if we are with them."[16]

Jerusalem means "City of Peace," but down through the centuries it has been anything but that. Although we continually "pray for the peace of Jerusalem" (Ps. 122:6), the answer seems long delayed. Holy Land violence like a simmering pot threatens to boil over at any moment.

Touring the Old City a few years ago, our group witnessed a riot at the Wailing Wall. A woman rabbi from Manhattan decided to pray at the men's section of the wall. The Orthodox rabbis went ballistic. Authorities locked down the gates, and it took a whole platoon of soldiers to quell the uprising. Needless to say, I was glad to get out of there.

My Palestinian friend, Hanna Massad, has chosen *not* to get out of there. Exiled in Jordan after the last persecution, Hanna, a Baptist pastor, keeps going back home to Gaza, one of the darkest places on earth. Amidst raging conflict and deep poverty, he ministers between two fires: militant Islamic aggression and harsh Israeli occupation.

Their Bible Society was bombed twice. The church was caught in the crossfire of a Hamas-Fatah shootout, critically injuring an employee. Arsonists torched the church's public library on three separate occasions. Extremists kidnapped Hanna's friend and coworker, Rami Ayyad, and executed him simply because of his bold Christian testimony. He left behind two precious children and a pregnant grieving wife.

Despite the persecution, Hanna and his wife, Suhad, chose to remain in the Middle East to serve their suffering friends, rather than leave for America where they hold citizenship. Standing with the vulnerable and poor, they stand with Jesus as they feed the hungry, clothe the naked, care for orphans, proclaim the gospel, encourage the saints, and train leaders.

There is not a hint of bitterness in this godly pastor. His tender spirit reminds me of Jesus who, approaching Jerusalem, wept and said, "If you, even you, had only known on this day what would bring you peace—but now it is hidden from your eyes" (Luke 19:42). The Palestinians and Israelis don't see it yet, but Hanna and Suhad offer the ellusive key to ending the Middle East conflict: Christ's peace.

Just as the nativity brought poor Jewish shepherds and rich Arabic wise men together in one humble place, so the gracious work of Jesus ripples forth from the Massads and other sincere Middle Eastern believers as they sow seeds of righteousness expecting a harvest of peace.

And some beautiful day, because of their holy love and courageous compassion, the words of Isaiah shall be fulfilled:

"Rejoice with Jerusalem and be glad for her, all you who love her; rejoice greatly with her, all you who mourn over her. For you will nurse and be satisfied at her comforting breasts; you will drink deeply and delight in her overflowing abundance." For this is what the LORD says: "I will extend peace to her like a river, and the wealth of nations like a flooding stream; you will nurse and be carried on her arm and dandled on her knees. As a mother comforts her child, so will I comfort you; and you will be comforted over Jerusalem." (Isa. 66:10–13)

"Blessed are the peacemakers: for they shall be called the children of God" (Matt. 5:9 KJV).

Follow my example, as I follow the example of Christ.

—1 Corinthians 11:1

# 12

# Influence

## Pour Out God's Power

Spiritual power is not given for the purpose of controlling others. We are empowered to empower them. God calls us to live and lead with open hands. Occasionally, people complain about power struggles in a congregation. Such conflicts are not so much a matter of power, but control. When leaders forget about empowerment, they get hung up on who gets to call the shots.

Like love, the more power you give away, the more you receive. The Holy Spirit's enduement provides abundant spiritual power to freely give away. Without the Spirit, we resort to grasping and hoarding.

My seminary professor friend, Tom Correll, stopped by my office one afternoon, bearing a book. "I heard you were preparing to teach a church leadership course and thought this resource might be helpful." He then handed me a copy of F. G. Bailey's *Humbuggery and Manipulation: The Art of Leadership*.[1]

"Humbuggery? Manipulation?" I protested. "That's not what I intend to teach. What does that have to do with church leadership?"

"More than we'd care to admit," Tom grinned. "Haven't you ever been humbuggered in church?"

I admitted that, indeed, I had been humbuggered on several occasions, and in a few regretable instances, even resorted to some manipulative arm-twisting myself. Of course, I didn't think of it that way. I assumed my encouragements to serve and give were altruistic. Occasionally though, those enlisted in my glorious causes wind up feeling bamboozled, wondering, "How on earth did I get into this?"

Humbuggery is what leaders do when they fail to rely on the Holy Spirit's guidance.

## Two Influence Paths

"The true measure of leadership," as John Maxwell said, "is influence—nothing more, nothing less."[2] Leadership is demonstrated by one's ability to persuade and influence others. Some pastors vehemently protest this principle. Fearing capitulation to business methods, they've overreacted by crafting a "smallness theology." For them, organizational excellence is an evil to be avoided like the plague, and any measure of influence is suspected as inauthentic. Rather than striving to grow as leaders, it's much easier to sit around and quack, "We may not be doing anything, but at least we have well-defined reasons."

Maxwell was right: Leadership is influence. If you are not influencing, you're not leading regardless of how cleverly you rationalize. There are, however, two distinctly different paths we can take to exert this influence: the humbuggery path and the holy love path.

Due to human nature a bit of both resides in us all, but one path or the other will dominate. We follow the holy love path only through intentional effort, and we resort to humbuggery when we're not fully flowing with genuine spiritual leadership. "The mind of sinful man is death, but the mind controlled by the Spirit is life and peace" (Rom. 8:6).

The church desperately needs Spirit-directed leaders, but they're hard to find. Humbuggery, the much easier path, appeals to the flesh and attracts many more voyagers. Paraphrasing Robert Frost, "Two leadership roads diverged in a wood, and I took the one most travelled by and haven't made much difference."

## The Humbuggery Path

It's easy to get lost in the Northwoods. Hikers frequently get off the path and wander in the wilderness without realizing they're lost. I've done that a couple of times. The tundra is confusing. A few missteps and we're staring up the wrong tree.

Likewise, the complexities of church leadership can sidetrack unsuspecting pilgrims from holy love to humbuggery. What signs reveal that we have strayed from the highway of holiness (Isa. 35:8) in our leadership?

### Pushing

Some folks by temperament are pushy. I happen to be one of them. I'm a pleasant pusher, mind you; but I've learned that people don't appreciate being pushed, even if it's with a smile. Of course, everybody knows that. Shove the guy in front of you at the grocery store and you will have a scuffle on your hands, even if you're grinning. Why are we surprised, then, by the conflicts that break out at church when we attempt to push people into our way of thinking? Pushing always results in a fight.

I searched Scripture to see what it said about pushing people. The only instance I found was when they heaved wicked Jezebel out the window (2 Kings 9:33). Other than that, I can't find one verse that says it's OK to push people. Following Jesus' example, we are called to guide, not shove.

My cat doesn't react well to pushing. Neither does my dog, wife, or kids. How can I expect my congregation to respond differently? God's doors are always equipped with automatic openers. You don't have to pry or push. All you need is the courage to step through when they open. If you must push somebody, push yourself to be less pushy and more patient.

## Driving

Closely related to pushing is driving. A few years ago, I read a book that said effective pastors are ranchers rather than shepherds. I loved that idea. When I was a little kid, I enjoyed playing cowboys. I proudly wore my western gear: boots, holster, and hat. This book told me I could be a cowboy for Jesus.

I was disappointed when I checked the Bible and couldn't find a single verse in there about cowboys or ranches. It spoke a bit about shepherding, however, so I hung up my spurs and went back to tending sheep. Shepherds gently lead their sheep; they don't drive them. Leaders who drive their people usually drive them up the wall or right out of the church.

## Manipulation

Although people need to be properly motivated, they should never be manipulated. Manipulation is using people to build programs rather than using programs to build people. It is pressuring individuals through guilt, fear, flattery, or sympathy to do something against their will for your benefit.

Of course, sometimes people need to be motivated to do what they would rather not because it's best. Legendary NFL coach Tom Landry said the leadership challenge is "to get people to do what they don't want to do in order to achieve what they want to achieve."[3]

Motivation differs from manipulation according to the spirit of the leader, the attitude of the follower, and the big picture of why we're doing this.

### Cowardice

Sometimes cowardice is cleverly disguised as compassion. Patient forbearance is honorable as long as it's not motivated by fear.

Spiritual leadership must be compassionate, but that doesn't excuse us from making hard calls when they're needed. Weak leaders melt like butter when the heat is on. There is a time to be soft, but there is also a time to be firm. Greater leadership responsibility requires making hard calls. Inability to make difficult decisions severely reduces one's scope of influence. Under fire, I sometimes pray, "God, harden me against myself."[4]

We need holy boldness to do the right thing without shrinking back regardless of the risk.

### Catastrophizing

Some leaders make everything out to be worse than it really is. They scurry around like Chicken Little shouting, "The sky is falling!" I have observed that when leaders fret, people catch the fever and multiply it. Anxious fear breeds wild alarm contrary to the Spirit of peace. "God has not given us a spirit of fear, but of power and of love and of a sound mind" (2 Tim. 1:7 NKJV). As long as God is on the throne and your faith is still intact, everything is going to be alright.

## Propaganda

On the opposite end of the spectrum, others are tempted to make things seem better than they really are. When motives are untrue, the accompanying declarations won't be true either. The mouth speaks from the heart's fullness (Matt. 12:34). Promoting image without substance is manufacturing illusion. Whitewashing reality to create false impressions for appearance' sake is propaganda, pure and simple.

For instance, a family historian could not bring himself to say that Great Uncle George died in the electric chair. Instead he wrote, "George occupied a chair of applied electronics at an important government institution and was attached to his position by the strongest of ties. His death came as a great shock."[5] I suppose that's one way to put it.

# The Holy Love Path

We discover genuine spiritual authority only along the holy love path. Such authority cannot be grasped or demanded. It is not gained by human effort but only through surrender and Spirit fullness. This authority increases over time as holiness matures and is the secret to effective, sustained church leadership.

So how do spiritual leaders influence others toward Christ's agenda for his church?

## Personal Investment

Spiritual leaders don't hold back but put their shoulder to the work. They give it all for Jesus and others—and all means *all*. Ministry demands sacrifice that goes far beyond minimal expectations. Half-heartedness cloaked as "healthy boundaries" is inexcusable. Of course healthy churches need healthy pastors and that takes intentional boundary setting. However, we must not use boundaries to avoid responsibilities. No shirking allowed. Ironically, it takes more energy to avoid hard work than to give all you've got. So just go for it.

## Prayer

Prayer, as mentioned in a previous chapter, is our most important work and our greatest source of spiritual influence. Prayer opens doors that would never budge by any other means. When we work, we work; but when we pray, God works.

## Planning

The secret to effective church planning is to promote God's agenda rather than our own. Leaders should pray until they are united in discerning divine direction—then they need to get into gear and move toward that end. This takes strategic planning which is spiritual in nature despite what some folks believe. God's purposes require careful but courageous planning.

## Positivity

Holy love leaders bring positive energy to the situation through faith and hope. "Someone once asked me if I was a pessimist or an optimist," said Billy Graham, "and I replied that I was an optimist—because I had read the last chapter of the Bible."[6]

## Programs

Despite what some in the church are currently saying, God still uses programs and processes for his purposes. In fact, even the

folks who decry programs have them. One pastor friend was trying to describe the difference between his church and mine. "You
are a program church and we are a missional community," he said.

"Ah, but we're a missional community and you're a program
church too," I came back.

"No, we don't have programs," he said.

"Do you have specific time and place to meet?" I asked.

"Of course."

"Do you have any people helping you lead?"

"Sure."

"Do you ever spend money on ministry?"

"Yes."

"Then you have a program whether you call it that or not," I said.

Actually, the main difference is that he has a small, unstructured
program and I have a larger, more systematic one. But in the big
picture, we're both doing the same thing for the same reason.

The most important concern is making sure you're doing the right
stuff and that your program is a means and not the end. Are people
coming to Jesus and growing in grace as a result? Are we exalting
Christ and blessing the community? If not, kill the program.

## The Stewardship of Influence

Our influence is on loan from God, and therefore we must be
wise stewards of it and give an account of it. What does stewardship of influence mean?

### Position

Respected leaders, especially long-tenured ones, do not fully grasp
the influence they have because of their position. This credibility can

be leveraged to bring stronger support to those who are disempowered.

## Possessions

We can also influence the world through freely giving our resources. Ironically, many pastors believe in the generosity principle when it comes to receiving offerings, but they don't apply it to the church when it comes to giving money and people away for the greater kingdom good. Pastors ought to practice what they preach and apply their stewardship sermon points to the church vision, budget, and mission efforts because:

- "It is more blessed to give than to receive" (Acts 20:35).
- "God loves a cheerful giver" (2 Cor. 9:7).
- "Give, and it will be given to you" (Luke 6:38).

## Passion

Uncontrolled passion leads to selfishness and sin, but when bridled it can lead to great accomplishment. Nobody has ever achieved anything extraordinary without a good measure of oomph. "Our gospel came to you not simply with words, but also with power, with the Holy Spirit and with deep conviction" (1 Thess. 1:5).

## Perseverance

In the end, your influence will not be measured by how you started, but by how you finished life's race. Determine to finish well.

# Cowbells for Hermann

Hayward is home of the American Birkebeiner, North America's largest cross country ski race. Approximately nine thousand skiers come from almost every state and many nations to compete in this world-class event. Spectators line snow-covered Main Street, ringing cowbells and cheering weary skiers across the finish line.

For two decades, I've been a Birkie cowbell ringer.

A day or two before the Birkebeiner, I always pine a little, wishing I had pulled the skis from the rafters and joined the throng of brave souls testing the limits of their endurance. But as Birkie day arrives, I find myself content to ring cowbells. After all, if everybody skied the Birkie, there wouldn't be anybody left to cheer.

Normally we ring in the elite skiers who finish first. Usually the winner is some Olympic European who hardly broke a sweat. I'm always impressed.

The best part of the race, though, is the middle of the afternoon, when all of the ordinary folks—lawyers, cooks, plumbers, and preachers come in. For them, it's a painful struggle for survival. I wipe sentimental tears and ring my bell with vigor.

It was shortly after dusk a few years ago when Hannah asked if we could go back down to the finish line.

"The race is over now, honey," I tried to explain.

"Please?" she pleaded. "It might not be over yet."

So against all odds, we packed up our cowbells and headed to Main Street. We arrived to see a busy crew removing snow and shutting down everything.

"See, we're too late," I began, when a worker with a walkie-talkie suddenly waved frantically and shouted, "Wait! Wait! There is one more skier coming in!"

Sure enough, long after all the other racers had hung up their skis, ninety-one-year-old Hermann Nunnemacher crossed the finish line. Midway in the race, Hermann fell and fractured four ribs, but he got back up and kept plodding forward!

With the crowds of spectators long gone, Hannah and I were the only cowbell ringers left—so we rang them for Hermann. We rang them with all our might!

For a few minutes, the workers stopped to shout and cheer. Some passersby also joined in the magical moment. Hermann crossed the finish line, and we all cried.

A reporter happened upon the scene and shoved a microphone toward Hermann. "You finished the race! How do you feel about that, Mr. Nunnemacher?"

Through cracked lips, the poor old guy croaked, "I hurt."

The next Wednesday, Hermann's picture graced the front page of *The Sawyer County Record*, the only time in history when the guy who finished last made the headline.

In life, ministry, and the Birkebeiner, it's not how you start but how you finish that counts. "I have fought the good fight, I have finished the race, I have kept the faith" (2 Tim. 4:7).

And God placed all things under his feet and appointed him to
be head over everything for the church, which is his body,
the fullness of him who fills everything in every way.

—Ephesians 1:22–23

# 13

# **Saturation**

## Go Be the Church

Our worship attendance plateaued after several years of sustained
growth, so a concerned pastor friend approached me. He was trying
to help, but it felt like Bildad the Shuhite (Job's comforter). "Aren't
you concerned about saturation?" he intoned. "After all, Hayward
is a very small town. Maybe you're at the spot where you're not
going to reach anymore people. There are only so many fish in the
pond, you know."

Saturation?

I'd never considered it, but now that the S-word was spoken,
it sank like a brick in my spirit. I went home depressed and told
Cathy, "Brother Bildad thinks we've hit saturation. We're not
going to grow anymore. I guess we'll have to spend the rest of
our days twiddling our thumbs and propping up the people we've
already got."

"It's God's church, not yours," Cathy reminded me. "Your job is to plant, water, and weed. The harvest is up to him. Don't fret about it. I'm sure he still has plenty of reaping for you to do." I wasn't quite convinced.

The next morning I found myself moaning to God about our saturation. "Why did you stick me with this?" I complained.

Then the light bulb clicked on. The word *saturation* means to be filled and overflowing. Do I want my people to be saturated and overflowing with God's presence, promise, peace, and power? Absolutely. Are they there yet? Not quite. There's still plenty of work to do. Do I desire our congregation to saturate the community with compassion, blessing, righteousness, and the influence of holy love? You bet. Has this been accomplished? Not yet. Plenty of work on that front too. Are there still people in our community lost without Jesus? Ten times more than the capacity of all the sanctuaries in town combined. Do we quit picking berries just because the easy ones are already plucked? No way. Do we stop fishing when the biting is slow? Not on your life. There's still plenty of work to do.

As long as one person remains unreached in our community, then our church isn't big enough. We must never settle. A single lost sheep means keep on seeking. Our task isn't close to completion. And what about reaching the world? Untold millions remain untold. We have not even begun to penetrate the darkest places. For God so loved the world, he sent his Son . . . and now he's sending us!

The next time a worried pastor asks if saturation concerns me, I'll say, "Absolutely. It's what I've been praying for. Bring it on!" After all, "revival," according to evangelist Duncan Campbell, "is a community saturated with God."[1]

## The Melting

In April after the long winter, our Northwoods community experiences "the melting." Warm, spring sunbeams turn the vast snow blanket into slush. Everything outdoors gets soppy. Ice dissolves. Rivers flood. Creeks overflow. Roads become streams. The melting snow fills every nook, cranny, and crevice. You can't step anywhere without putting your foot in it.

You might call that saturation.

This is my prayer for the church. I long for the day when the "frozen chosen" are so melted together by God's holy love that it permeates everything around them. I pray that revival rivers will rise as heaven's floodgates open. This saturation will impact and transform every nook, cranny, and crevice of culture as God's people go forth in holy love.

I long for the day the church demonstrates God's presence so vibrantly that we'll knock the "sin" right out of Wisconsin—so it will just be called Wiscon, or better yet, Wiscon-grace, for where sin abounds, grace abounds all the more!

## The Tide Is Coming In

A few years ago, Cathy and I travelled to Wales and visited Loughor, the epicenter of the mighty 1904 Welsh Revival. God used Evan Roberts, a humble young man who simply prayed, "Bend me," to be the catalyst for this powerful movement of the Holy Spirit.

Sparked in a small youth meeting, the revival quickly spread through the community. Within a few days, all the local churches were packed nightly with seekers. Multitudes embraced Roberts' simple message:

1. Confess all known sin.
2. Deal with and get rid of anything "doubtful" in your life.
3. Be ready to obey the Holy Spirit instantly.
4. Confess Christ publicly.[2]

Before long, the entire region was saturated by the revival. Bible sales increased dramatically; taverns sat empty; coal miners stopped swearing, returned tools they had stolen, and sang hymns as they worked; sports became unimportant; and the crime rate dropped.[3]

Within a year, one hundred thousand people in Wales were converted to Christ, and the revival extended over Europe and across the sea to many nations. Over a century later, we continue to reap the results of this powerful movement.

The old sexton of Moriah Chapel where everything began gave us a tour. He told about the great outpouring and how his parents were among the early converts. When I asked how things were going at the church today, he shook his head and tearfully lamented the decline in attendance, participation, and mission. "This church saw so many glorious things," he wept, "and now we have a mere handful of committed members."

Later he drove us by the tidal basin where a rivulet of water barely trickled. "This is the site of the second highest tide in the world," he exclaimed. "Right now it is just a small stream, but later today, the tide will come in and fill the entire basin. It's a spectacular sight to behold." He continued, "Spiritual fervor in our land has diminished to hardly a trickle."

Then with a determined gleam in his eye, he declared, "But we're praying, longing, and believing. And someday . . . someday . . . the tide is coming in!"

Like the Moriah sexton, I too am praying, longing, and believing for the same thing in my community, reflecting the words of Salvation Army founder, William Booth,

> O ocean of mercy, oft longing I've stood
> On the brink of thy wonderful, life giving flood!
> Once more I have reached this soul cleansing sea . . .
> I will not go back till it rolls over me.
> The tide is now flowing, I'm touching the wave,
> I hear the loud call of the Mighty to Save;
> My faith's growing bolder, delivered I'll be . . .
> I plunge 'neath the waters, they roll over me.[4]

## Playing Church

We won't experience this mighty outpouring as long as we're content with playing church.

When I was a kid, I loved to play church. I lined teddy bears up the stairs and preached to them. One day Daddy came down the steps and walked over my bears, interrupting the worship service. "Hey!" I shouted, pointing my finger like Nathan the prophet, "Quit stepping on my congregation!"

Lately the Devil has been stepping on too many congregations. Defeated churches pose little danger to the minions of darkness. Ministry motions without the Spirit are lifeless pretendings.

I wonder how much money, time, and energy is expended just playing church. It seems to me that every pastor and leader ought to regularly ask these vital questions:

- What is God's mission for our church in our community?
- Are we investing fully in this cause?
- Do our programs, activities, budget, and schedule reflect God's priorities?
- What tangible difference is our church making beyond its walls?
- How can we start something new?

The answers to those questions will reveal whether you are intentionally engaged in the mission or just fiddling around.

All "church playing" pastors and boards should be fired—fired up for God, that is. Too much is at stake for us to settle for leaders who won't lead and pastors who won't pastor. A congregation's job is not to provide positions, but to reach the community for Christ.

Lukewarm leaders pose the planet's greatest threat to spiritual renewal. If we don't possess the real thing, how can we possibly bring it to others?

For a while, the H1N1 flu virus caused great alarm. Many people caught it, and everybody heard about it. My prayer is for an outbreak of H2N2: Hope and Holiness for our Neighbors and the Nations. I hope it goes viral, spreading across town and around the world, impacting so many lives that even those who don't get it will hear about it.

## My Journey to Missional Benedictions

### Thanks for Coming to Church

In my early years of ministry, I always ended church with, "You're dismissed." That's the way my dad did it. During my upbringing, I heard over 3,500 "You're dismisseds" at the end of worship services, so naturally, it was ingrained in me to do the same thing.

One day George called and asked if he could take me to lunch. I thought he was just being nice, but he had a burr in his britches.

"As a diehard Presbyterian, it drives me up the wall when you say, 'You're dismissed' at the conclusion of the services. I'm standing there waiting for a blessing, something inspiring to take home with me, and you say, 'You're dismissed.' There are only two places where I've heard those words: in the classroom and when I got fired from my job. Neither memory is pleasant. I wish you would give us a good, rich benediction—but if you can't do that, would you at least say, 'Thank you for coming to church'?"

Benedictions don't come naturally to me, so in deference to George, I quit saying, "You're dismissed" and started saying, "Thank you for coming to church."

### Thanks for Being the Church

That went fine for a few years, until Mark called and asked if he could meet with me.

"As a theology professor, it bothers me when you say, 'Thank you for coming to church' at the conclusion of the services. It fosters a sense of American consumerism, like 'Thank you for shopping at Walmart.' The congregation needs to be challenged to see we're not doing God some big favor by showing up. Besides, church isn't just a place to go to; it is who we are. Would you please consider saying something different?"

"How about if I finish with something about *being* the church?"

"Well at least that's an encouragement," Mark smiled.

So for the next couple of years, I concluded each service with, "Thank you for being the church."

## Go Be the Church

That went along great until Andreas called and asked if he could meet with me.

Andreas, a bright-eyed missionary from Germany, has developed an effective Native American ministry in our area. I call him the German Shepherd.

"As a missional community leader, it concerns me when you finish the services with 'Thank you for being the church.' You're inadvertently saying that 'being the church' is what we are inside the building. People might think that if they've sat in a pew, sung a few songs, and listened to a sermon, they've been the church. That's pretty passive. Christians need to understand that they are called to do the kingdom stuff—reaching out to the lost, praying for the sick, caring for the poor, and proclaiming the gospel of the kingdom outside the church walls."

"You're right!" I agreed.

After that, I began ending the worship services with a challenge: "Go be the church. We have worshiped and prayed together. We have heard God's Word. Our hearts have been filled with grace. Now take it out into the community. We have been blessed to be a blessing. Go be the church."

I continued to say, "Go be the church," until, while working on this book, I had a follow-up conversation with theology professor, Mark.

After I shared my journey from "You're dismissed" to "Go be the church" with Mark, he said, "I think there's still something more."

The next day he sent me the following excerpt from McGrath's *Theology*, explaining the meaning of the phrase *the Mass*: "This term arose in the Latin-speaking western church during the third century. Its original meaning was 'dismissal,' referring to the send out of the congregation into the world after the service was completed."[5] At the bottom of the message Mark added, "So maybe you can come full circle in your "benediction narrative" to saying once again, "You're dismissed!"[6]

## The Church Distributed

What would happen if everybody took me up on the "go be the church, dismissed into the world" challenge? What if all our people became missionaries rather than members? What if they saw themselves as pastors instead of pew potatoes? What if they viewed all of life as ministry—bringing the blessing of holy love to others? Can you picture it?

One lady who understands said, "I am an undercover agent for Jesus Christ, cleverly disguised as a secretary."

With this mindset . . .

- Janet the kindergarten teacher is not just a school teacher. She is a pastor, and her twenty-two students are members of her congregation. She may be limited by law in what she says, but she can tenderly shepherd their hearts. She nurtures, blesses, and prays for them. There is no law against love.
- Jim the salesman is not just a salesman. He is a pastor, and his customers are the members of his congregation. Stepping into his daily appointments, he seeks ways to encourage and lift heavy hearts as an ambassador for Jesus.
- Don the football coach is not just a coach. He is a pastor, and the players are the members of his congregation. While teaching skills and teamwork, he also forges character through godly mentoring.

- Linda the nurse is not just a nurse. She is a pastor, and every patient is a member of her congregation. As she assists others, she brings a significant level of compassionate care that comes only through Christ's love.
- And the pastor is not just a pastor. He or she is an apostle— equipping, encouraging, and interceding for all the pastors out in the field, who were formerly benchwarmers.

Cultural Christianity has held the laity captive for too long. It's time to throw off the shackles, arise, and be the church! The urgent need requires a wholehearted response from us all.

## Doing the Real Stuff

It's time for pastors to quit being the "God-pros" and trust the people to do the real stuff. Sometimes by default we mistakenly assume that pastors are the only ones qualified to do meaningful ministry. When people buy into this, the members of the congregation are relegated to the uninspiring role of supporting cast. We turn high octane businessmen into bulletin distributors and suffocate our most capable leaders by sticking them on mundane committees. They were created to do so much more.

It's time to rethink how we do ministry on a daily basis and entrust our people with the most important pastoral moments. It's time to unleash the church.

## Overflow

Many sideline believers know their faith should be far more robust than participating in programs, consuming music, and donating money. Wholehearted engagement in Christ's mission ignites our hearts, captures our imagination, and transforms our community. Otherwise, it's just a form of godliness without the power.

God wants to do something special today. Are we ready to get out of the box and receive all he offers? The only hindrance is our reluctance. He stands ready to immerse our hearts with his presence. He calls us to live by faith in his promise. He is the source of our deepest contentment and peace. He is able to endue us with supernatural power.

This infilling saturates the heart, resulting in an overflow. Jesus does the work and we go with the flow. We pour out his presence with compassion. We pour out his promise with blessing. We pour out his peace through righteousness. We pour out his power through spiritual influence.

God stands ready to flood our hearts with his presence, promise, peace, and power so mightily that it overflows all the boundaries and saturates the entire congregation, then the community, and then the world!

Holy love flows in. Holy love pours out.

Serve in the overflow. This is our glorious mission. Don't settle for halfhearted religion. The floodgates of relevant revival are opening. Are you ready to plunge in?

Here is love, vast as the ocean,
Lovingkindness as the flood,
When the Prince of Life, our Ransom,
Shed for us His precious blood.
Who His love will not remember?
Who can cease to sing His praise?
He can never be forgotten,
Throughout Heav'n's eternal days.

On the mount of crucifixion,
Fountains opened deep and wide;
Through the floodgates of God's mercy
Flowed a vast and gracious tide.
Grace and love, like mighty rivers
Poured incessant from above,
And Heav'n's peace and perfect justice
Kissed a guilty world in love.

In Thy truth Thou dost direct me
By Thy Spirit through Thy Word;
And Thy grace my need is meeting,
As I trust in Thee, my Lord.
Of Thy fullness Thou art pouring
Thy great love and power on me,
Without measure, full and boundless,
Drawing out my heart to Thee.[7]

## Church Dismissed

So go. Go be the church in the strength and power of the Lord. Be a blessing wherever you go. Share holy love all along the way, and the God of peace will be with you.

You're dismissed!

# Notes

## Chapter 1

1. Vance Havner, *The Best of Vance Havner* (Old Tappan, N.J.: Fleming H. Revell Co., 1967), 100.
2. Thomas C. Oden, *Pastoral Theology: Essentials of Ministry* (New York: HarperCollins, 1983), 26.
3. H. B. London Jr. and Neil B. Wiseman, *Pastors at Greater Risk* (Ventura, Calif.: Regal, 2003), 172.
4. Peter Drucker, as quoted by Dennis Rainey in "Encouraging Your Pastor," accessed June 10, 2011, http://www.familylife.com/site/apps/nlnet/content3.aspx?c=dnJHKLNnFoG&b=3584679&ct=4638373.
5. Harvey A. Herman, "Anorexia of the Soul: A Burnout Checklist for Pastors," accessed June 10, 2011, http://www.enrichmentjournal.ag.org/200902/200902_000_Anorexia_of_soul.cfm.
6. Craig Groeschel, "The Christian Atheist," as reported by Perry Noble, accessed June 10, 2011, http://www.perrynoble.com/2009/05/15/four-points-of-attack-part-four-your-ministry-methods.
7. Wesley L. Duewel, *Ablaze for God* (Grand Rapids, Mich.: Zondervan, 1989), 74.
8. A. B. Simpson, quoted in Mrs. Charles E. Cowman, *Springs in the Valley* (Grand Rapids, Mich.: Zondervan, 1997), 10.
9. H. B. London, Jr. and Neil B. Wiseman, *Pastors at Risk: Help for Pastors, Help for the Church* (Wheaton, Ill.: Victor, 1993), 179.
10. Neil Cole, *Organic Church: Growing Faith Where Life Happens* (San Francisco: Jossey-Bass, 2005), 162.

11. Corrie ten Boom, *Don't Wrestle, Just Nestle* (Old Tappan, N.J.: Revell, 1978).

12. Over twenty years ago, my friend Tom Raven brought the quote back from England, where he learned it from African immigrants.

13. Henri J. M. Nouwen, *The Return of the Prodigal Son: A Story of Homecoming* (New York: Doubleday, 1992), 115.

14. Thomas R. Kelly, *A Testament of Devotion* (New York: Harper-Collins, 1941), 46.

15. Rob Evans, The Donut Man, accessed June 10, 2011, http://donut man.com/?page=scrapbook.

## Chapter 2

1. I heard this story from my father. Attempts to discover the author have been unsuccessful.

2. Thomas Merton, *No Man Is an Island* (New York: Harcourt, Brace and Co., 1955), 24.

3. "Quotes about Revival," Leonard Ravenhill, accessed June 10, 2011, http://www.goodpassage.com/articles/quotes_about_revival.htm.

## Chapter 3

1. "God's Requirements for Revival: Humility," Rick Flowers, accessed June 10, 2011, http://www.sermoncentral.com/sermons/gods-requirements-for-revival-humility-rick-flowers-sermon-on-emotions- 42606.asp.

2. Research from Barna and Gallup consistently reveals that the lives of professing Christians are not much different than those who do not claim a relationship with Christ.

3. Jesus condemned the Pharisees for that kind of righteousness.

4. Henry David Thoreau, *Walden* (New York: Random House, 1950), 68.

5. "I Asked the Lord that I Might Grow," John Newton, accessed June 10, 2011, http://nethymnal.org/htm/i/a/iaskedtl.htm.

6. "Honest Dealing with God," Charles Haddon Spurgeon, Metropolitan Tabernacle Pulpit, accessed June 10, 2011, http://www.spurgeon.org/sermons/1241.htm.

7. John Wesley, "The Important Question," *The Works of John Wesley*, 3rd ed. (Peabody, Mass.: Hendrickson, 1991), VI: 495.

8. ———, *Directions for Renewing our Covenant with God* (London: J. Paramore, 1781), 12.

9. Daniel J, Kadlec, "Me Generation Becomes We Generation," *USA Today* (August 2, 2006) accessed June 10, 2011, http://www.usa

today.com/ news/opinion/editorials/2006-08-02-we-generation-edit_x.htm.

10. Brian Mosley, "5 Reasons We Are Outsourcing Our Faith," blog entry by Brian Mosley, February 8, 2010, http://brianmosleyblog.com/2010/02/08/5-reasons-we-are-outsourcing-our-faith.

11. Frank Wedekind, Quotes Archive, accessed June 10, 2011, http://www.quotesarchive.com/authors/w/frank-wedekind/quotes/god-made-man-in-his-own-image-and-man.

12. I borrowed this idea from my son Ryan.

## Chapter 4

1. William Shakespeare, *Julius Caesar*, act 4, scene 3.

2. R. A. Torrey, *Revival Addresses* (Chicago: Revell, 1903), 148.

3. "O the Deep, Deep Love of Jesus," S. Trevor Francis, accessed June 10, 2011, http://www.cyberhymnal.org/htm/o/t/othedeep.htm.

4. *Lord, Save Us from Your Followers*, directed by Dan Merchant (New York: Virgil Films and Entertainment, 2010), DVD.

5. American Board of Commissioners for Foreign Missions, the first American Christian foreign mission society, was founded in 1810.

6. Ernest Hemingway, "Big Two-Hearted River," *The Complete Short Stories of Ernest Hemmingway* (New York: Simon & Schuster, 1987), 163.

7. Dallas Willard, "Understanding Spiritual Transformation" (lecture, Bethel Seminary, Roseville, Minn., May 20, 2003).

8. John Wesley, "The Scripture Way of Salvation," *The Works of John Wesley*, 3rd ed. (Peabody, Mass.: Hendrickson, 1991), VI: 53.

9. Phoebe Palmer, as quoted in James Gilchrist Lawson, *Deeper Experiences of Famous Christians: Gleaned from Their Biographies, Autobiographies and Writings* (Anderson, Ind.: Warner, 1911), 378.

10. Wesley L. Duewel, *Ablaze for God* (Grand Rapids, Mich.: Zondervan, 1989), 68.

11. This phrase, used as the title of Peterson's outstanding book (Downers Grove, Ill.: InterVarsity, 2000), was borrowed from philosopher Frederick Nietzsche.

12. Mother Teresa and Brian Kolodiejchuk, *Come Be My Light: The Private Writings of the Saint of Calcutta* (New York: Random House, 2007), 169, 192.

13. "Luther's *Anfechtungen*: Setting for the Reformation," Richard P. Bucher, accessed June 10, 2011, http://www.orlutheran.com/html/anfecht.html.

14. Kathleen Norris, *Acedia & Me: A Marriage, Monks, and a Writer's Life* (New York: Penguin, 2008), 5.

15. Charles Spurgeon, "The Minister's Fainting Fits," in *Lectures to My Students* (London: Passmore & Alabaster, 1875), 167–178.

## Chapter 5

1. Corrie ten Boom, *Each New Day* (Minneapolis, Minn.: Revell, 1977), September 25.

2. Thomas Cook, *New Testament Holiness* (London: Wertheimer, Lea & Co., 1902), 168.

3. This is my modernized adaption of a poem my father taught me. Author anonymous.

4. George Gallup and Jim Castelli, "Americans and the Bible" *Bible Review,* June 1990, http://members.bib-arch.org/publication.asp?PubID=BSBR&Volume=6&Issue=3&ArticleID=18.

5. Albert Mohler, "The Scandal of Biblical Illiteracy: It's Our Problem" (blog), October 14, 2005, http://www.albertmohler.com/2005/10/14/the-scandal-of-biblical-illiteracy-its-our-problem.

6. Marilyn Sewell, "Questions of Faith," *Portland Monthly*, January 2010, http://www.portlandmonthlymag.com/arts-and-entertainment/category/books-and-talks/articles/christopher-hitchens/1.

7. Scot McKnight, "Apologetics in a Postmodern World 1," *Jesus Creed: Exploring the Significance of Jesus and the Orthodox Faith for the 21st Century* (blog), September 13, 2010, http://www.patheos.com/community/jesuscreed/2010/09/13/apologetics-in-a-postmodern-world-1.

## Chapter 6

1. Steinbeck borrowed this line from Shakespeare's *Richard III*, for the title of his 1961 novel.

2. Roy B. Zuck, *The Speaker's Quote Book: Over 5,000 Illustrations and Quotations for All Occasions* (Grand Rapids, Mich.: Kregel, 2009), 156.

3. Thomas Watson, *The Art of Divine Contentment* (London: L.B. Seeley and Sons, 1829), 18.

4. Ibid., 28–29.

5. This idea came from a chapter in Roy Hession, "The Mote and the Beam," in *The Calvary Road* (England: Book Trust, 1950), http://www.christianissues.biz/revival.html.

6. This line was the inspiration of the hymn "Leave It There" by Charles A. Tindley, accessed June 10, 2011, http://www.cyberhymnal.org/htm/l/e/leaveitt.htm.

7. John Piper, *Brothers, We Are Not Professionals: A Plea to Pastors for Radical Ministry* (Nashville: Broadman & Holman, 2002), 45.

8. Stormie Omartian, *Prayers for Emotional Wholeness: 365 Prayers for Living in Freedom* (Eugene, Ore.: Harvest House, 2007), 18.

9. Leonard Sweet and Frank Viola, *Jesus Manifesto: Restoring the Supremacy and Sovereignty of Jesus* (Nashville: Thomas Nelson, 2010), 128.

10. Ibid.

11. Bill Hybels, *Holy Discontent: Fueling the Fire That Ignites Personal Vision* (Grand Rapids, Mich.: Zondervan, 2007), 29.

12. Billie Joe Daugherty, *Knocked Down, But Not Out* (Shippensburg, Pa.: Destiny Image, 2006), 105–106.

13. The poem inscribed on the stained glass window was written by Mary F. Bulls.

## Chapter 7

1. Wesley L. Duewel, *Ablaze for God* (Grand Rapids, Mich.: Zondervan, 1989), 78.

2. *The Discipline of the Wesleyan Church 2008* (Indianapolis, Ind.: Wesleyan Publishing House, 2008), 5785.

3. From John Hoffman, Presbyterian pastor from California. Used with permission.

4. Leslie D. Wilcox, *Power from on High: A Study of the Enduement of the Holy Spirit in Relation to Entire Sanctification* (Salem, Ohio: Schmul, 1979), 14. I have taken the liberty to update the language to reflect the NIV rather than KJV.

5. Ibid., 14–15.

6. Oswald J. Smith, *The Enduement of Power* (London: Marshall, Morgan & Scott, 1970), 43.

7. John Wesley, *The Works of John Wesley*, 3rd ed. (Peabody, Mass.: Hendrickson, 1991), I: 103–104.

8. Curtis C. Thomas, *Practical Wisdom for Pastors: Words of Encouragement and Counsel for a Lifetime of Ministry* (Wheaton, Ill.: Crossway Books, 2001), 209.

9. Dallas Willard, *The Divine Conspiracy: Rediscovering Our Hidden Life in God* (San Francisco: HarperCollins, 1998), 143.

10. John Wesley, "The Lord Our Righteousness," *The Works of John Wesley*, 3rd ed. (Peabody, Mass.: Hendrickson, 1991), V: 234.

11. R. A. Torrey, *Why God Used D. L. Moody* (Chicago: Revel, 1923), 53.

12. Richard Ellsworth Day, *Bush Aglow: The Life Story of Dwight Lyman Moody Commoner of Northfield* (Philadelphia: The Judson Press, 1936), 137.

## Chapter 8

1. Tom Albin, "Questions God Asks" (lecture, Beulah Holiness Camp, El Dorado, Illinois, July 27, 2009).

2. Cliff Barrows, "Passion for Souls, Passion for Prayer," *Decision Magazine*, April 1, 2005, http://www.billygraham.org/articlepage. asp?ArticleID=537.

3. E. M. Bounds, *Purpose in Prayer* (Radford, Va.: Wilder, 2008), 7.

4. Brother Lawrence, *The Practice of the Presence of God* (Grand Rapids, Mich.: Revell, 1967), 12.

5. Andrew Murray, *Abide in Christ* (New Kensington, Pa.: Whitaker House, 1979), 104.

6. E. M. Bounds, *Preacher and Prayer* (Winona Lake, Ind.: Light and Life, 1946), 11.

7. Wesley Duewel, *Touch the World through Prayer* (Grand Rapids, Mich.: Francis Asbury, 1986), 208.

8. Oswald Chambers, "Why Can I Not Follow You Now?" *My Utmost for His Highest*, January 4, 2011, http://utmost.org/why-can-i-not-follow-you-now.

## Chapter 9

1. Edwin Markham, "Outwitted," in *The Shoes of Happiness and Other Poems* (New York: Doubleday, 1915), 1.

2. Henry Moore, *The Life of Mrs. Mary Fletcher* (London: J. Kershaw, 1824), 165–166. John referred to her by the nickname Polly.

3. Mark Batterson, *Primal: A Quest for the Lost Soul of Christianity* (Colorado Springs: Multnomah, 2009), 169.

4. Carey Landry, "Only a Shadow," Copyright © 1971 by Carey Landry. Recorded 1973, on "Hi God," OC Publications. Used with permission.

5. Richard J. Foster, *Celebration of Discipline: The Path to Spiritual Growth* (San Francisco: HarperCollins, 1998), 189.

6. John Wesley, "The Character of a Methodist," *The Works of John Wesley*, 3rd ed. (Peabody, Mass.: Hendrickson, 1991), VIII: 341–342.

7. Batterson, 17.

8. Kevin Myers (panel discussion, Wesleyan Pastors' Gathering, Jacksonville, Fla., January 6, 2011). Kevin quoted Andy Stanley, "One, Not Everyone" (sermon, North Point Community Church, Alpharetta, Ga., January 2, 2011).

9. Elisabeth Elliot, *Through Gates of Splendor* (Wheaton, Ill.: Tyndale, 1981), 20.

10. Margaret Wheatley, *Finding Our Way: Leadership for an Uncertain Time* (San Francisco: Berrett-Koehler, 2007), 218.

11. Adelle M. Banks, "Study: Youth See Christians as Judgmental, Anti-Gay," *USA Today*, October 10, 2007, http://www.usa today.com/news/religion/2007-10-10-christians-young_N.htm.

12. Sigurd F. Olson, *Listening Point* (Minneapolis: University of Minnesota Press, 1986), 8.

13. Dave Isay, *Listening Is an Act of Love: A Celebration of American Life from the StoryCorps Project* (New York: Penguin, 2007).

14. Dr. Jo Anne Lyon shared this heart-touching story in a video update from the Board of Wesleyan General Superintendents shortly after the devastating Haiti earthquake in January 2010.

15. Sharon Rhodes Wickett, United Methodist pastor from Claremont, California, sharing what she observed while attending the annual conference of the Methodist Church in Freetown, Sierra Leone, February 1984.

## Chapter 10

1. Indiana Wesleyan University was called Marion College back in those days.

2. Brian Lusky, "Overflow," recorded December 2009, on *Who Can Stand*, Brian Lusky, http://brianlusky.com/wp-content/uploads/2009/11/overflow-e.pdf. Used with permission.

3. Rebecca Manley Pippert, *Out of the Saltshaker & into the World: Evangelism as a Way of Life* (Downers Grove, Ill.: InterVarsity, 1980), 15.

4. Ruth A. Tucker, *Left Behind Churches in a Megachurch World: How God Works through Ordinary Churches* (Grand Rapids, Mich.: Baker, 2006), 199–200.

5. Maya Angelou, accessed June 13, 2011, http://thinkexist.com/quotation/i-ve_learned_that_people_will_forget_what_you/341107.html.

6. Gary Smalley and John Trent, *The Blessing* (Nashville: Thomas Nelson, 1986), 24.

7. Christian Smith, *Souls in Transition: The Religious and Spiritual Lives of Emerging Adults* (Oxford: Oxford University Press, 2009), 152–153.

## Chapter 11

1. Charles W. Keysor, *Our Methodist Heritage* (Elgin, Ill.: David C. Cook, 1973), 15.
2. John Wesley, *The Works of John Wesley*, 3rd ed. (Peabody, Mass.: Hendrickson, 1991), I: 103.
3. ———, "Salvation by Faith," *Works*, V: 7.
4. Teddy Roosevelt used this idea in his December 6, 1904, speech before Congress, saying, "Unrighteous wars are common, and unrighteous peace is rare; but both should be shunned." Willis Fletcher Johnson, ed., *Addresses and Papers of Theodore Roosevelt* (New York: The Unit Book Publishing, 1909), 228.
5. See "Marking the Way to Freedom," accessed June 13, 2011, http://www.themissionrestaurant.com/history.html. The "human touch" was, more specifically, seven faces carved into the wall that are now on display at the Onondaga Historical Association.
6. Freedom's Hill Church has been reconstructed at Southern Wesleyan University in Central, South Carolina.
7. Laura Smith Haviland, *A Woman's Life-Work*, 5th ed. (Grand Rapids, Mich.: S. B. Shaw, 1881), 566.
8. The two Haviland towns are in Kansas and Ohio.
9. Anna Howard Shaw with Elizabeth Jordan, *The Story of a Pioneer* (New York: Harper & Brothers, 1915), dedication.
10. Tony Casey, a Wesleyan pastor from South Carolina, has done extensive research on this subject.
11. J. W. Vess, Letter to the General Superintendent, *The Wesleyan Methodist*, May 23, 1962.
12. Wesley, "Preface, List of Poetic Works," *Works*, XIV: 321.
13. Leonard Sweet and Frank Viola, *Jesus Manifesto: Restoring the Supremacy and Sovereignty of Jesus* (Nashville: Thomas Nelson, 2010), 112.
14. These thoughts were sparked by Bob Whitesel's outstanding book, *Spiritual Waypoints: Helping Others Navigate the Journey* (Indianapolis, Ind.: Wesleyan Publishing House, 2010), 14–16.
15. "Top 10 Facts about Modern Slavery," Free the Slaves, accessed June 13, 2011, http://www.freetheslaves.net/Page.aspx?pid=375.

16. Bono, "Transcript: Bono Remarks at the National Prayer Breakfast," *USA Today*, February 2, 2006, http://www.usatoday.com/news/washington/2006-02-02-bono-transcript_x.htm.

## Chapter 12

1. F. G. Bailey, *Humbuggery and Manipulation: The Art of Leadership* (Ithaca, N.Y.: Cornell University Press), 1988.
2. John Maxwell, *The 21 Irrefutable Laws of Leadership: Follow Them and People Will Follow You* (Nashville: Thomas Nelson, 1998), 11.
3. Tom Landry, *An Autobiography* (New York: HarperCollins, 1990), 269.
4. J. Oswald Sanders, *Spiritual Leadership: Principles of Excellence for Every Believer* (Chicago: Moody Press, 1994), 53.
5. Several different versions have been floating around for years. "Family Tradition," accessed June 13, 2011, http://www.funnyclean jokes.com/family-tradition.
6. Billy Graham, "Spiritual Growth Topics," accessed June 13, 2011, http://www.billygraham.org/spiritualgrowth_topics.asp?prid=2&tid=14.

## Chapter 13

1. Bryan Galloway, "A Reminder of Duncan Campbell's Definition of Revival," *Pray for Revival!* (blog), August 1, 2011, http://pray forrevival.wordpress.com/category/a-people-saturated-with-god.
2. "1904 Revival," Evan Roberts, accessed June 13, 2011, http://www.1904revival.com/Evanroberts-extract.html.
3. Sue Wampner, a student in my March 2011 evangelism class, researched the Welsh Revival and wrote a paper on the subject, noting these effects and more.
4. William Booth, "Boundless Salvation," accessed June 13, 2011, http://www.cyberhymnal.org/htm/b/o/boundles.htm.
5. Allister E. McGrath, *Theology: The Basics* (Malden, Mass.: Blackwell, 2008), 144–145.
6. Mark Jalovick, e-mail message to author, March 23, 2011.
7. William Rees, "Here Is Love," accessed June 13, 2011, http://www.cyberhymnal.org/htm/h/e/herelove.htm.